SOCIAL PSYCHOLOGY AND PHYSICAL ACTIVITY

Harper's Series on Scientific Perspectives of Physical Education,
Rainer Martens, Editor

SOCIAL PSYCHOLOGY AND PHYSICAL ACTIVITY

Rainer Martens
University of Illinois

Harper & Row, Publishers
New York   Evanston   San Francisco   London

Sponsoring Editor: Joe Ingram
Project Editor: Ralph Cato
Designer: Michel Craig
Production Supervisor: Stefania J. Taflinska

Social Psychology and Physical Activity

Library of Congress Cataloging in Publication Data
Martens, Rainer 1942–
    Social psychology and physical activity.

    (Harper's series on scientific perspectives of
physical education)
    Bibliography: p.
    1. Physical education and training—Psychological
aspects. 2. Sports—Social aspects. 3. Socialization.
4. Social interaction. I. Title. (DNLM: 1. Physical
education and training. 2. Psychology, Social.
HM251 M377s)
GV342.M258   613.7'01'9   74-7674
ISBN 0-06-044231-X

CONTENTS

SERIES PREFACE

As has occurred in several other fields, the knowledge explosion in physical education and its collateral sciences—the biological and behavioral sciences—warrants a different approach for conveying introductory material. Traditionally, a basic course has used a single text that superficially covers everything, but sacrifices depth. The alternative is a text that covers one area in depth, but ignores many essential topics. Neither approach is adequate. Physical education has become too diverse for any one individual to write about all areas with complete authority. The developments in the behavioral and biological areas of the field have been too rapid.

The Scientific Perspectives of Physical Education series attempts to remedy the instructor's dilemma of choosing between breadth and depth. It is composed of five volumes, representing the fields of physiology, kinesiology, psychology, social psychology, and sociology. In that order, the series moves from a biological emphasis to a social emphasis. Each science is included because of its obvious relationship to the other fields, as well as for its growing body of knowledge, which is a function of the amount of scholarly activity occurring within it. And, of course, each field is included because of its relevance for the diversified physical education profession.

The Scientific Perspectives of Physical Education series, then, is a direct outgrowth of the scholarly activity occurring in physical education and collateral sciences. Physical educators are now realizing the importance of reaching the introductory, as well as upper-level, student with high-quality, well-written, interesting material. Rather than material based on speculation and conjecture, information that highlights the continuing and exciting search for new knowledge is being sought. This series is our attempt to place such material in the hands of physical educators.

Each volume is written by an individual actively engaged in research in this field. The approach of the series has been to focus on the reciprocal relationship between physical activity or sport and the subject area. More explicitly, the influence of physiological, biomechanical, psychological, social psychological, and sociological variables on physical activity or sport are considered, as well as the influence of engaging in physical activity or sport on these same variables.

Although the material is written for the introductory student in physical education, it presumes that the student has a basic understanding of the various disciplines represented. Within each area we hope to convey what is known today, what is currently being studied, and what needs to be understood. Emphasis is placed on content rather than method. Although method dictates the quality of the content, the authors assume responsibility for discriminating between quality and lesser research. Documentation of material has been used sparingly, primarily for recent work, in order to retain readability.

By no means is the series to be considered definitive within each area or for the entire field. Much of our knowledge is incomplete; our understandings are limited. But it is necessary to remember that the acquisition of knowledge in each area is an ongoing process. Each author has attempted to tell it as it is, not as what he hopes or conjectures it to be.

The series offers some flexibility because each volume is self-contained and may be used separately, or as a partial or complete set for a foundations course. Although written for the introductory undergraduate student, dependent upon the student's background and the curriculum, the series may be useful at more advanced levels.

Rainer Martens

PREFACE

The behavior of people involved in physical activity, particularly sport, has long been of interest. For many years we have speculated about how one player "psychs out" another in a contest, or how sport is an outlet for suppressed emotions, or how participation in sport develops leadership. Not until recently have we begun to turn our speculations into legitimate scientific inquiry.

The study of man's behavior in relation to his social environment when involved in physical activity—the "social psychology of physical activity"—is the subject matter of this book. We will attempt to illuminate the nature of influence relationships among individuals, whether on individual-to-individual, individual-to-group, or group-to-group basis, while they are involved in physical activity. We shall see in Chapter 1 that this field, although closely allied to sport psychology and the sociology of sport, is nevertheless distinct.

The intent of this book is to provide a structured purview of the social psychology of physical activity. To accomplish this goal, the major concepts and experimental evidence are discussed by moving from the basic to the more complex social psychological processes. This volume is by no means a comprehensive exposition of the entire field. Instead, the material herein reflects the interests of major divisions of social psychology as they relate to physical activity. In some cases, however, such as Chapter 3 on observational learning, physical education has largely ignored an important area. Material has therefore been included in the text with the expressed hope that future practitioners and researchers will give more serious attention to the topic. It has also been necessary to make some arbitrary divisions between the social psychology of physical activity and the sociology of sport. At the fringes of any discipline the boundaries that separate it from another field become obscure. The decision has been made to include the broad field of group dynamics (or small group research) within the *Sociology of Sport* text in this series, rather than within this text.

This book does not seek to apply social psychological knowledge to the solution of social problems as they occur in sport and physical activity, nor does it attempt to show how physical activity or sport can solve man's myriad social problems. This book attempts to present the social psychology of physical activity *as a science* and to present its *current* state of development as accurately as possible. Within these pages there are no "laws of social behavior" that are appropriate to use when teaching or participating in physical activities—simply because *no such laws have been established or verified*. In accordance with the current status of the field, many more questions are posed than resolved, and emphasis throughout is directed toward establishing a valid perspective about the application of scientific methodology to the study of human social behavior. Although some areas have received considerable experimental attention and have shown promising theoretical developments, other areas of immense importance to physical education have been sadly neglected. Consequently the subject matter herein tends to be uneven in quality and quantity, reflecting the unfortunate unevenness in both quality and quantity of the actual research in various areas.

An attempt, however, has been made to distinguish between what is known by means of the scientific method and what is conjectured to be known. This author has been critical about some areas of research—or, more appropriately, of *conjecture* presented as fact—perhaps as an overreaction to the inaccurate generalizations so frequently heard. The intent in being critical, however, is to be constructive rather than destructive. One can only begin to make progress in understanding our social environment by recognizing what is and what is not legitimately known.

The book is divided into three parts. Part I is an orientation to the general field of social psychology and an introduction to social psychology as it relates to physical activity. Part II introduces four social processes that are almost always operative when involved in teaching or participating in physical activities—social facilitation, observational learning, social reinforcement, and competition. Beyond analyzing the structure of these processes, we specifically discuss the influence they have on motor behavior. Part III is directed at understanding the process by which one becomes a "socially competent" person— the process of socialization. This part of the book begins by considering how various agents, agencies, and cultural forces operative in the socialization process influence motor behavior. Of course, particular emphasis is placed on the role that sport, games, and general physical activities have in the development of socially competent individuals. Specific attention is given to the relationship between physical activity and interpersonal competence, aggression, attitudes, and personality.

Many of the topics discussed in Parts II and III have been of longstanding interest to physical educators, although usually these topics have been perceived as being isolated. *Social Psychology and Physical Activity* integrates this subject matter under the disciplinary umbrella of social psychology. While it has been enjoyable to attempt to separate fact from fiction, it will even be more enjoyable to observe the development of new facts in the near future.

Rainer Martens

PART I

SOCIAL PSYCHOLOGY: AN OVERVIEW

The objective of Part I is to introduce
students to the field of social psychology.
In one all too brief chapter we try to provide
enough background to enable the student
to appreciate the content and method of
social psychology. The content of social
psychology is emphasized through the more
prevalent social psychological theories or
orientations. In our review of methods
used in social psychological research we
emphasize the approach of contemporary
American experimental social psychology.
The discussion of method presented in the
last part of Chapter 1 is not intended to
be an exhaustive discussion of this topic;
this would require at least several large
volumes. Instead, an attempt is made to
highlight those methodological concerns

that are unique or prevalent in social psychology and that will help the reader interpret this text. For those with no background in social psychology, the reading of Chapter 1 should be complemented by one of the many available introductory social psychology texts.

CHAPTER 1

INTRODUCTION TO SOCIAL PSYCHOLOGY

In this first chapter we have much to do. In order to establish some flexible boundaries, we shall survey the field of social psychology by indicating the content and method of this field. We also shall define physical activity and related terms and discuss the relationship between social psychology and physical activity. And to help us understand the methods of inquiry used by social psychologists we will take a brief look at social psychological theories.

SOCIAL PSYCHOLOGY AND PHYSICAL ACTIVITY DEFINED

Social psychology is the science that seeks to understand the "hows" and "whys" of human social behavior. As a science, social psychology is of very recent vintage; as a subject of interest it is ancient yet persistent. Our interest in social behavior is particularly keen today because our physical technology has advanced so rapidly that we have not managed satisfactorily to keep pace with the social impact of these changes; that is, our physical technology has transcended our social technology. Physical engineers have learned how to build splendid machines, to transform matter into huge quantities of energy, and to make creative use of our physical resources for human consumption. Just as we need these developments by physical engineers, we also need social engineers to help us control the uses of these technological developments. Physical technology has thrust us into diversified social relations, demanding that we play many roles and modify our behavior to meet a variety of demanding situations. Thus as physical technology continues to move ahead and as the complexity of our society increases we must understand how people affect one another. Social psychology is the science that seeks such understanding by investigating the influences that produce regularities and diversities in human social behavior. Social psychology is one of the behavioral sciences that is developing our social technology and provides the basis for training social engineers.

To define social psychology more explicitly we must consider both its content and its method. Stated simply, its content is concerned with the individual's relationships with his social environment, and its method is that of modern psychology as an empirical science. Although social psychology's content is ancient, its method is new and changing. Such everyday occurrences as a father scolding his son for mischievous behavior, a physical educator teaching students how to swim, students demonstrating on a college campus, a physical therapist working with a patient, two friends meeting at a football game, and countless similar encounters constitute the subject matter of social psychology. These single isolated events are of no scientific interest in and of themselves, but the regularities in these encounters—their similarities and differences—are important in understanding human social behavior. Therefore one of the basic assumptions permeating all of the behavioral sciences is

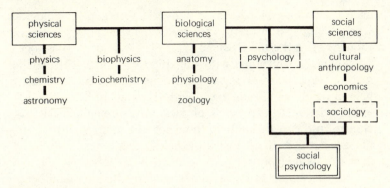

Figure 1.1. The evolution of social psychology.

that human behavior is *not capricious* but is subject to some discoverable laws of cause and effect.

McGrath (1964) has stated that social psychology is "the scientific study of human behavior as influenced by the presence, behavior, and products of other human beings, individually and collectively, past, present, and future" (p. 1). Although the scope of social psychology is broad, its commitment is quite clear. It has a conviction that the mutual relationships between the individual and his social context can be properly studied with the methods and underlying philosophies of science similar to those upon which the natural sciences have developed.

In reference to the content of social psychology, the central concern of this field is with the process of *social influence*. Social influence occurs whenever one individual responds to the actual or implied presence of one or more others. Social influence relationships may occur in one of the following three forms: (1) person-to-person interaction, (2) person-to-group interaction, and (3) group-to-group interaction. In reference to the method of social psychology, the scientific process involves (1) the collection of carefully made observations, (2) the ordered integration of these observations to permit the statement of general principles describing the logical patterns into which they fall, and (3) the utilization of these general principles to predict future observations. Later in this chapter we will consider the methods of social psychology in greater detail.

As can be seen from Figure 1.1, in the evolution of the sciences, psychology emerged as a hybrid, being part biological science and part social science. Social psychology can be thought of as the social science part of psychology. Thus social psychology is concerned with the study of human behavior in relation to a person's social environment, and the remaining field of psychology is concerned with the study of human behavior in relation to a person's physical environment. Social psychology also is tied closely to the fields of sociology and anthropology, but is distinct from these fields because first, its interest is in the *individual* as a participant in social relationships, and second, its emphasis is on *understanding* the social influence processes underlying these relationships. It is particularly important in specifying the scope of social psychology to remember that its basic unit of analysis is the *individual*. By contrast sociologists and anthropologists take as the basic unit of analysis the social or cultural system in which the individual lives (e.g., the group, institution, society). Obviously one field cannot be studied without reference to the others, but the social psychologist's approach is to bring the individual into focus against a background of the society—not vice versa.

Social psychology also is distinctive in that with people, unlike objects or things, psychological events can take place on both sides of the relationship. For example, if you kick a rock it cannot react to you, although you may react to the kick! But if you kick another person, he may get angry and kick you back. When you encounter a friend on the street both of you perceive, feel, and think of each other in certain ways. Furthermore each of you is aware that the other can perceive and act, and that these perceptions and actions can refer to you. This capacity to be aware of one another and to be affected by one another forms the intriguing but complex subject matter of social psychology.

Now let us look at social psychology as related to physical activity. The term *physical activity* is used here because of its nonspecific meaning. Our nomenclature to describe human movement and the settings in which movement occurs is quite limited. Physical activity, however, is a general term with few fences around it. It does not distinguish between, nor does it eliminate, either motor learning or performance.[1] It does not imply a particular setting in which movement may occur. It may occur in a very formal setting such as a highly organized professional sport contest or it may occur in an informal setting such as a group of children playing in a sandpile. Physical activity does not imply a particular purpose for movement either. It may be physical activity for the purpose of increasing or maintaining fitness or it may be for the purpose of acquiring another goal, such as money or prestige. Then, too, it may appear to be nonpurposeful behavior. Thus physical activity, including sport, generally conveys the notion of observable human movement occurring in a wide variety of settings.

We have already seen how social psychology is distinct from the other behavioral sciences. Similar distinctions need to be made between what has been referred to as sport psychology, sociology of sport, and social psychology of physical activity. Sport psychology is as yet an ill-defined field. Logically, one would expect sport psychology to be concerned with the relationships between both the physical and social environment and human behavior occurring in a sport context. In reality, however, sport psychology has not only included sport but has come to mean a psychology of movement or motor behavior. Currently, three areas of scientific investigation are active in sport psychology—motor learning, motor development, and social psychology. Both motor learning and motor development have been rather clearly recognized components of sport psychology. In addition to being concerned with how motor skills are acquired and how human movement develops, sport psychologists have been interested in the personality of athletes, the attitudes of students in physical education, the motivation of players, and with aggression in sport and competition in general. Few sport

---

[1] Motor learning refers to the acquisition of a motor skill, which is an inference made based on changes in performance. Motor learning then is a relatively permanent change in motor behavior as a result of practice, and this learning is not directly observable. Motor performance refers to a single skilled movement sequence. Performance is also used in a general way to infer that initial learning has occurred and changes in performance are no longer dramatic.

psychologists, however, have viewed these social variables as forming a subfield within sport psychology. Thus one purpose of this text is to show how these social variables, when placed under the umbrella of social psychology, form an important, unified, and systematic area. It should be noted, however, that because motor learning, motor development, and social psychology each study movement in contexts other than sport, the name sport psychology, which has been used to encompass these fields, is a misnomer.

As indicated in the Preface, the relation between social psychology and physical activity is two-sided. On the one hand we will focus on the influence of social psychological variables on motor skill acquisition and performance, and on the other we will consider the influence of involvement in physical activity, particularly sport, on social psychological variables. In focusing on the former, we will consider the influence of an audience, the use of social reinforcement, the influence of a model, and the impact of competition. We will discuss the latter by considering such variables as personality, attitudes, and aggression. To clarify, the first focus asks, for example: "What is the influence of competition on hitting a baseball?" The second asks: "Will playing competitive baseball for several years change my personality?"

To distinguish social psychology of physical activity from sociology of sport we can follow the general discipline distinction. Sociology of sport does not focus on the individual; instead it is concerned with sport group processes, cultural influence on sport or sport as part of the culture, and with institutions and organizations concerned with sport. Social psychology is also interested in these features, but only from the perspective of how they influence the individual or how the individual influences them. Also, the social psychology of physical activity is not limited in its concern to a sport context, which is the case for the sociology of sport.

THEORIES IN SOCIAL PSYCHOLOGY

In studying human social behavior, social psychologists moved from a social philosophy approach to a social empiricism approach, and more recently to a social analysis approach.

(Hollander, 1967.) Speculation and conjecture characterize social philosophy, the earliest approach to the study of human social behavior. The related methods of introspection and retrospection heavily influenced the early recorded thoughts on human social behavior. Systematic observations of social behavior were not made.

Discontent with the social philosophy approach grew as the natural and biological sciences began to make significant developments through empiricism. In the nineteenth century, social psychologists reacted to the lack of rigor in the social philosophy approach by adopting the empiricism approach for the study of human social behavior. Social empiricism is characterized by its systematic data gathering, but it lacks the direction of theory. Although this approach is superior to the social philosophy approach, social empiricism is often guided by philosophical speculation.

The most advanced approach is the social analysis approach, which emphasizes theory development based upon systematic observations and the controlled testing of theoretically derived hypotheses. As a twentieth century development, the social analysis approach goes beyond merely describing the phenomenon by seeking to understand the "hows" and "whys" of human social behavior through the verification of relationships among variables. The use of the social analysis approach has earned social psychology the distinction of being a social science. Unfortunately, much of the research related to the social psychology of physical activity falls into the category of social empiricism and not social analysis. Thus we will give considerable emphasis to the use of theory in understanding human social behavior.

We can think of a theory as representing a blueprint. We would not attempt to build a school or a house without a plan, a detailed blueprint of the projected structure. A blueprint shows the relationship of the major features of the building to one another. The rooms, the windows, the doors, the plumbing, and the electrical system must be planned in relation to the other features of the building. A theory of human social behavior has features analogous to doors and windows, and so on. These are called constructs. A theory represents a set of interrelated constructs that presents a systematic view of phenomena by specifying the relation between these constructs, with the purpose of explaining and predicting the phenomena. (Kerlinger, 1967.) As it is necessary to define the material and units of measurement on a blueprint, it is also necessary to define the constructs of a theory by describing how they are measured. Everyone knows what an 8-foot wall looks like, and it is easy to determine if it is actually 8 feet. But what is anxiety, or group cohesion, or an attitude? How are they defined? How are they measured? We can best define and measure such constructs by the use of a theory. In the subsequent chapters of this monograph, this point will be illustrated.

Many theories about human social behavior exist. These theories are convenient ways of organizing experiences; they permit us to digest vast amounts of empirical data with few propositions; they enable us to see implications and relationships not evident from the data alone; and they are a stimulus and guide for further empirical investigation. (Shaw and Costanzo, 1970.) Some theories are broad, explaining a wide array of phenomena, while other theories are narrow in scope, explaining the relationship among few variables. Most theories of human social behavior can be classified under one of three theoretical systems—psychoanalytic, cognitive, and behavioristic. Below we briefly describe and compare each theoretical system.

Psychoanalytic Theories

Man is a *homo volen*—a striving man—according to psychoanalytic theories. Man has unconscious inner urges that are expressed as drives and emotions. He is a battleground between his animal nature and society, as represented by his family. Psychoanalysis is concerned with the metamorphosis of man from a biological, pleasure-ridden organism at birth to a socialized, reasoning adult at maturity. (Deutsch and Krause, 1965.) According to Freud, the father of psychoanalytic theories, psychoanalysis was several things at once: (1) a system of conducting inquiry into human functioning, (2) a system of psychotherapy, and (3) a theory of human behavior. (Shaw and Costanzo, 1970.)

Psychoanalytic theories place emphasis on the libido, a source of hydraulic pressure, which acts as a motivational force exerting itself through a variety of channels within the person, directing specific behaviors. Considerably more emphasis is placed on the source of energy than on its direction. Strong emphasis is also placed on the importance of unconscious influences on behavior, and conscious experience is interpreted in the light of inferences made about unconscious and motivational forces. The importance of unconscious influences on behavior is reflected in Freud's emphasis on dreams, embarrassing mistakes of everyday life, and wit as expressions of lawful psychological processes common to man.

Psychoanalytic theories minimize the importance of the physical and social environment in influencing the person's behavior, emphasizing that man is active rather than reactive. Consequently man is viewed as the creator of culture rather than the product of cultural forces. Historically, psychoanalytic theories have played a major role in conceptual development in the following general areas of social psychology: (1) socialization of the person, (2) personality development, (3) family structure and dynamics, and (4) the sources of aggressive behavior. Although a major influence in social psychological theorizing in the past, psychoanalytic theories have received little direct experimental attention through the years. Although at one time the most influential theory in social psychology, psychoanalytic theories today are the least influential of the three major theoretical systems.

Cognitive Theories

In cognitive theories the emphasis is on the central processes of the organism to explain behavior. In recent years a number of cognitive theories have emerged like branches on a tree, with the trunk being Gestalt psychology. The major concern of Gestalt psychology is with the process of perception and perceptual organization. Thus as derivatives of Gestalt psychology, cognitive theories view man as concerned primarily with the development of an organized and meaningful view of his world. Man is a Homo sapien—a thinking man. Kurt Lewin derived his field theory from Gestalt psychology, which emphasizes the motivational forces associated with perceptual organization.

Increasingly the concern with the motivational properties

associated with a search for cognitive structure has shifted the focus of cognitive theories. Initial interest in cognitive theories centered on the ways social phenomena are cognized. Today, however, the concern is with *how* cognitive processes are the causes or underlying dynamics of social behavior. Cognitive theorists rely heavily on verbal behavior as the source of data, but are also making use of overt behavioral observations. From consistencies in patterns of such overt action, the cognitive theorist infers the existence of patterns and processes of cognitive organization.

Unlike the psychoanalytic theories, cognitive theories minimize the importance of unconscious determinants of behavior, although they do not deny the existence of unconscious factors. Conscious experience, however, is of the highest importance. Furthermore because cognitive theories emphasize the organization of experience, the environmental factors that give rise to experience are especially important. Little distinction is made between social and cultural elements of the environment and the nonsocial or physical elements.

Gestalt and field theory have been the basis for a number of recent influential cognitive theories in social psychology such as Festinger's theory of cognitive dissonance (1957), Heider's theory of cognitive balance (1958), and Newcomb's theory of communicative acts (1953). The common features of these theories center on the idea that an organization, or structure of beliefs and attitudes, or of interpersonal relations may be imbalanced, incongruous, or dissonant; and that when imbalance occurs, there is a tendency to change one's beliefs, attitudes, or behavior until they are in balance. These and other cognitive theories are currently very influential in social psychology.

Behavior Theories

The behaviorist is concerned primarily with how behavior is acquired and emitted; man is viewed as *homo mechanicus*— a reactive man. Homo mechanicus is a machine analogous to a complex computer that may be programmed to link certain kinds of input to certain kinds of output. The early development of behavior theories can be traced back to Thorndike and

Pavlov and to their conviction that behavior is determined primarily by its immediate consequences of pleasure or pain. Early behaviorism minimized the importance of the organism's inherent internal structure and placed total emphasis on external variables or the person's environment in determining behavior. Arising from the early work of Hull (1943) and Miller and Dollard (1941), behavior theories began to exert increasing influence on social psychology. As a result, in the 1950s social psychologists became increasingly interested in such variables as social motivation, social learning, and social rewards and punishments.

During this period a new behaviorism began to emerge, with increasing emphasis on the social and cultural milieu. Associated with the emergence of what has been called neobehaviorism was a concern with the central processes that give coherence and versatility to the input from the environment and the output to the environment. Thus neobehaviorism is the beginning of a merger of cognitive and behavior theories.

In comparison to psychoanalytic and cognitive theories, traditional behavior theories are considered very "hard shelled." Staunch behaviorists reject any concepts for theory building as inappropriate if they do not permit empirical observation. The neobehaviorists, however, have mellowed on this conceptual rigor. Although the role of conscious experience in human behavior is minimized, the neobehaviorists at least give secondary consideration to the individual's cognitive experience.

Which theoretical position is best? The question cannot be answered directly. The use of theories in social psychology is eclectic; no one theory appears to be clearly superior. For example, cognitive theories appear to be better for explaining attitude formation and change, and behavior theories seem to more satisfactorily explain social learning by observation (imitation). A good theory must be logically consistent and must be in agreement with known data. Theories are considered better than others if they are also as parsimonious as possible, if they are consistent with related theories, if they are interpretable in terms of the real world, and if they serve a useful purpose. In terms of current influence, psychoanalytic theory has little influence, cognitive theories have a strong and steady influence, and behavior theories have increased their influence. Now we shall look briefly at how data, the building blocks of theories, are obtained scientifically.

METHODS IN SOCIAL
PSYCHOLOGICAL RESEARCH

Social psychology is committed to the scientific method, otherwise it would not be a science. The scientific method is simply a set of rules for achieving certain goals. The goal of social psychology is to understand the process of social influence. To gain this understanding we must first describe individual social behavior by observing it, and then discover why it is the way it is, or explain it. Description is the empirical goal of social psychology; explanation is the theoretical goal. American social psychology in particular has a strong commitment to empiricism; that is, to the scientific method of deriving an understanding of man's experience and behavior from direct observation. In this section we shall examine how these observations are made, but first we must acquaint ourselves with the language of the scientist.

Two kinds of truth preoccupy the empirical scientist. The first truth is *reliability* of the observations made and the second is the *validity* of the observations. Reliability is concerned with the dependability, the consistency, and accuracy of the observations made. Validity is concerned with the question: Are we measuring what we think we are measuring? High validity is indicated by the observations being comprehensive, durable, and meaningful.

In studying human behavior the behavioral scientist works with concepts. Concepts are abstractions formed by generalizations from observations. Competition, for example, is an abstraction about behaviors in social situations. Various observations about two individuals interacting may be labeled competition. A *construct* is a concept but additionally it means being invented or adopted for a particular scientific purpose. To measure constructs we *operationally define* them; that is, we assign meaning to the construct by specifying the activities or operations necessary to measure the construct.

Many observations are made by means of *experiments*. An experiment is "a situation in which one observes the relationship between two *variables* by deliberately producing a change in one and looking to see whether this alteration produces a change in the other" (Anderson, 1966, p. 21). Variables are commonly labeled *independent* and *dependent*. An independent variable is the one that the experimenter deliberately changes to cause an effect. The variable that is examined to see whether it is affected by changes in the independent variable is called the dependent variable. An independent variable is the antecedent, the cause; the dependent variable is the consequence, the effect.

In evaluating an experiment the problem of *internal* and *external validity* is of major importance. Internal validity asks: Did the independent variable have some significant effect on the dependent variable in this specific instance? Internal validity is concerned with establishing a causal relationship between the experimental variables. External validity asks: To what extent can the results of this study be generalized? External validity is concerned with determining the extent that the relation holds in contexts other than the initial one. (Campbell, 1957.)

Research Settings

In making observations of human social behavior, social psychologists use one or more of the following methods that occur in different settings: field study, field experiment, laboratory experiment, and computer simulation. The sources of data used within these various settings include direct observations, subjective reports, attitude assessment, sociometric methods, content analysis, sample surveys, and cross-cultural methods. We shall first outline the settings in which social psychological research is conducted and then review some sources of data and specific research techniques.

Field Study

Investigations that are made in real-life natural settings that do not attempt to manipulate or influence the individual under observation, are known as field studies. Field studies rely primarily on sources of data such as the analysis of existing records and documents (content analysis), surveys, and observational techniques. The field study has the advantage of having high external validity because of its real-life atmosphere. The field study also has the positive attribute of getting beneath the surface of phenomena because it is concerned more with detailed observation and less with sampling procedures. The disadvantages of a field study are that it is difficult to determine cause and effect relationships because the independent variable is not manipulated by the investigator (known as ex post facto research), it is difficult to find appropriate field settings for the study of some problems, and often it is very difficult to make unobtrusive observations. That is, the observational method used in a field study obtrudes on the normal behavior of the subject, who then changes his behavior atypically. Together with the inadequate sampling methods usually used, field studies frequently have low internal validity.

Field Experiment

A field experiment, like a field study, also occurs in a natural, real-life social setting. Unlike a field study, though, in a field experiment the experimenter manipulates the independent variable in some way. Both field studies and field experiments use existing natural social groups; e.g., a basketball team. An example of a field study would be the observation of a professional basketball team's games to determine the frequency with which white and black team members pass the ball to each other. An example of a field experiment would be the same situation, but we manipulate the lineup so that the ratio of white and black players on the court varies according to our desire. The independent variable manipulated by the experimenter is the ratio of black and white players. The dependent variable is the frequency of passes between black and white players. The crucial methodological problem of field experiments is to find ways to carry out the manipulation of the independent variable.

The advantages of a field experiment are that the findings are not artificial; therefore, they have high external validity. Field experiments, as compared to field studies, permit a more unequivocal determination of causal relations; that is, internal validity is considerably better than in field studies because the independent variable is under the control of the experimenter. Leading social psychologists are currently advocating greater use of field experiments because of this advantage. They are even suggesting that sport is an excellent field situation for conducting experiments into social processes. Field experiments are particularly well suited for studying methods of social change, social processes, and social learning.

The primary disadvantage of the field experiment is its difficulty in execution. Field experiments often require much time and therefore may be quite expensive. The greatest threat to the destruction of the field experiment is the imposition of the measuring process. To overcome this problem social psychologists have recently shown much interest in the use of unobtrusive measures. (Webb et al., 1966.) Unobtrusive measurement means making observations of human behavior without the observed persons reacting or changing their behavior due to the observational process. Many sport and physical activity situations appear to offer excellent opportunities for obtaining unobtrusive measures.

Laboratory Experiment

A laboratory experiment is exactly what the name implies. It is a rigorously controlled test of a specific hypothesis occurring in an artificial or contrived setting. Therefore the study is usually high in internal validity but may be deficient in external validity because of its artificial laboratory environment. Laboratory studies are commonly used when the experimenter is well acquainted with the major independent variables that govern the behavior he wishes to study. Laboratory experiments in social psychological research typically manipulate a few critical variables that are of experimental interest and hold other variables constant. Laboratory experimental research in social psychology was less prevalent than other methods for many years, but today it is the dominant mode of social psychological research. The popularity of laboratory experiments, occurring within the last 15 years, is attributed to the precision gained by this method and the success with the method. Its relatively late emergence, however, is a result of the relatively late developments in experimental methodology; including developments in experimental design, statistics, and high-speed computers.

An important limitation of the laboratory experiment is the difficulty in making social variables powerful enough in the laboratory; that is, manipulating the independent variable to approximate reality. For example, it is very difficult to create the same kind of stressful situation in a laboratory when studying the influence of competitive stress on motor performance, as compared with the actual stress experienced immediately before a wrestling match or playing in a championship football game. Consequently, internal validity frequently is gained only at the expense of external validity.

Computer Simulation
Computer simulations are primarily mathematical models of human social behavior. They frequently become quite complex and therefore computer analysis becomes essential. Computer simulations, unlike the methods above, are closed models in that all variables are included in the model. Both the independent and dependent variables are built into the formulation of the simulation model. Consequently, the model is not tested on human subjects, but information from previous testing is fed to the computer, and based on the form of the model, consequences of certain behaviors are determined on a probability basis. At the present time computer simulation is relatively unknown to many social psychologists and has not come into wide use. Its primary advantages are that it can handle large quantities of data and it is economical. Its primary disadvantage is that its accuracy depends on what the programmer feeds into the model.

These four settings or classes of methods are neither totally distinct from each other nor are they completely interchangeable. Instead they are complementary to one another. Based upon the investigator's knowledge of the phenomenon and his interest, he will select the method best suited to his particular problem. In making this decision the researcher considers how these variables fall on several continua. For example, at the field study-end of the continuum the methods are more concrete, real, but loosely controlled, while at the computer simulation-end the methods are more abstract, artificial, but highly controlled. Each method has distinct advantages and certain limitations. Most thorough investigations of some phenomenon will use more than one method.

Sources of Data

The direct observation of human social behavior is one of the primary sources of data because it frequently can be unobtrusive. Observations can be made from concealed positions such as behind one-way mirrors, and they can be recorded on film or video-tape for later analysis. The major problem with observational methods is defining the unit of observation. Many systems have been devised for classifying behavior, each having advantages and weaknesses. Some systems will have as few as 4 or 6 categories of behavior and some have as many as 200 or 300. Another difficulty with direct observational systems is that they require interpretive skill on the part of the observer. Often the skill varies considerably, resulting in inconsistencies from one observer to the next, producing low reliability.

Perhaps the greatest source of all social psychological research data is obtained from a person's report of his own behavior. These subjective reports are obtained primarily by interviews and from psychological tests. These sources of data have the tremendous advantage of being easy to obtain, but have a number of severe limitations. Respondents to interviews and psychological tests may misunderstand questions, they may attempt to misrepresent themselves, and the test may be constructed so that individuals cannot really express their true opinion.

Another source of data is the procedures used to assess attitudes. Attitude assessments differ from other psychological tests in that they do not induce the individual to report his attitudes directly as he is aware of them. Instead, attitude scales attempt to have the individual express judgments about some phenomenon from which attitudes can be inferred.

A source of data that is unique to social psychology and sociology is sociometry. Sociometric procedures are used for measuring various facets of interpersonal relationships, which is their distinctive feature. Rather than assessing individual attributes, sociometric methods measure the relationships between individuals. The simplest sociometric method is the sociogram, which is simply a graphic representation of sociometric observations. These observations can be made by an observer or they can be obtained by questioning the individual. For example, each member of a group could be asked to indicate his two best friends in the group, or the two least liked persons, or any other interpersonal attribute. Because sociograms quickly become unmanageable as the size of the group increases, other sociometric methods have been developed. With the availability of high-speed computers, sociometric indices and sociomatrices have become very popular. Although space prohibits further discussion of these complex methods, they have become important tools for social psychologists. (See Kerlinger, 1967, for a complete discussion of sociometric methods.)

Content analysis is another source of data that relies primarily on the interpretation of existing documents and records. In social psychology, content analysis has been used primarily to study verbal and nonverbal communication patterns.

PART II

BASIC SOCIAL PROCESSES AND MOTOR BEHAVIOR

When we mention motor learning or motor skill acquisition, many physical educators think about such things as knowledge of results, kinesthetic feedback, fatigue, massed versus distributed practice, transfer of training, and retention. Obviously it is important to understand how these variables influence motor learning and performance, but it is also important to know the influence of social variables on the learner. In Part II we shall examine four social influence processes and their relation to motor behavior. In Chapters 2 and 3 we shall look at *social facilitation* and *observational learning*, respectively; in Chapter 4 we discuss the role of *social reinforcement*; and in Chapter 5 we examine the fascinating topic of *competition*.

Although considerable scholarly interest has centered on the study of motor behavior in the last 30 years, throughout this period little attention has been paid to the social environment in which motor learning and performance occur. It is almost as though motor behavior occurs in a social vacuum; but of course it does not. The neglect of the social environment, unfortunately, dictates that in the next four chapters we ask more questions rather than provide answers. For example, in the observational learning chapter, we have very little direct experimental evidence to present, but because the topic is so relevant and has been ignored so long, we cannot omit it simply because researchers have. Thus throughout Part II we draw upon the theory and research done in the general field of social psychology and the extant research specific to motor behavior to provide the best possible explanation. It is painfully evident that our explanations are incomplete, but the importance of the subject matter warrants the risk of partial explanation in the hope that it will stimulate others to provide more complete answers.

CHAPTER 2

SOCIAL FACILITATION

It was 1897 when Norman Triplett, a bicycle enthusiast and social scientist, noticed that bicyclists appeared to perform better in a race against another person than in a race against time. Others with whom he shared this thought disagreed. Therefore Triplett decided to conduct an experiment to prove he was correct. He tested individuals over a 25-mile course in both situations and compared their times. Indeed those competing against another individual consistently averaged over five seconds per mile faster than those individuals racing against time. Triplett's (1898) study was recognized as the first experimental investigation in the field of social psychology and he auspiciously referred to this phenomenon as the dynamogenic factor in pacemaking. Although today we may be tempted to call it the "rabbit effect," the term *social facilitation* has become popular.

Actually the term *social facilitation* has been used in two ways. Narrowly defined, social facilitation refers to any *increment* of individual behavior resulting from the presence of another individual. In the experimental work that followed the lead of Triplett, several studies found facilitory effects. Meumann (1904), for example, noticed that each time he entered the laboratory his students would markedly improve their performance on a finger ergograph as compared to when they worked alone. Similar facilitory effects were found by researchers using both verbal and simple motor tasks. (Travis, 1925; Dashiell, 1930; Allport, 1920.)

Social facilitation narrowly defined, however, explains only one part of the influence of the presence of other individuals. A number of early investigations also found social *impairment* or inhibitory effects. For example, the presence of several spectators disturbed and interfered with the learning of nonsense syllables and a finger maze. (Pessin, 1933; Pessin and Husband, 1933; Husband, 1931.) And still other studies found no difference at all between individuals performing alone or in the presence of others. As is very common in the behavioral sciences, the results were equivocal—not decisive—or so it appeared. As is commonly the case when scientists reach an impasse, interest in an area wanes and the problem waits for a new idea, method, or approach to solve the problem. And so it was with social facilitation.

PRESENCE OF OTHERS

The spark that rekindled interest in social facilitation came from Robert Zajonc (1965), who not only gave the area some consistent nomenclature but also showed with ingeniousness that the results were not so inconsistent. Zajonc popularized the term *social facilitation* as a general term referring to both positive and negative effects as a consequence of the presence of others, although its initial use in this context should be credited to Allport (1920). Zajonc incorporated two experimental conditions known as the audience effect and the coaction effect under the social facilitation rubric. The audience effect refers to the behavioral effects occurring from the presence of passive spectators. The coaction effect refers to the behavioral effects resulting from the presence of other individuals doing the same thing at the same time, but independently. A golf class in which each individual is practicing "chip" shots is an example of a coaction situation. A coaction situation is distinct from a cooperative situation, the latter requiring task interdependence. Both the audience and coaction situation may be competitive situations, but not necessarily. We shall have more to say about this when discussing competition.

Zajonc's (1965) ingenious reformulation of the social facilitation literature was made through the application of drive theory to this body of research. He noticed that the equivocality of this literature could be reduced by distinguishing between learning and performance. On simple tasks that required very little learning the presence of others resulted in response facilitation. However, on complex tasks (tasks that required considerable learning), response impairment occurred in the presence of others. Through drive theory research, it has been well established that increases in arousal tend to elicit the dominant response (the response more likely to occur) in a habit hierarchy of responses. That is, when an aroused individual is confronted with a stimulus that elicits a potential family of responses, the response that is stronger in the repertoire of responses is more likely to occur. Drive theory research has also shown that in *learning*, the dominant response tends to be the incorrect response, but when *performing* a well-learned response, the dominant response tends to be correct.

Zajonc was then able to provide some evidence that the presence of others increases arousal. This, of course, was the critical link in his reformulations. When it was made, the conclusion was obvious: The mere presence of others impairs learning because the aroused individual more frequently emits the incorrect response, but facilitates the performance of a well-learned task because the aroused individual more frequently emits the correct response.

AUDIENCE EFFECT

Zajonc's explanation stimulated new research on this old problem. Using the audience paradigm and verbal tasks, several studies supported Zajonc's explanation. (Cottrell, Rittle, and Wack, 1967; Ganzer, 1968; Zajonc and Sales, 1966.) But does an audience have a similar effect when learning and performing motor skills?

To answer this question we need to distinguish between simple and complex motor skills and between learning and performance. Furthermore a valid test of Zajonc's hypothesis should determine whether or not the presence of others is indeed arousing. Using drive theory, which was the basis of Zajonc's reformulation, a complex motor task is one in which a stimulus tends to evoke a number of competing responses. This simply means that although there may be one or several correct responses, there also may be a number of incorrect responses. The complexity of the task is dependent upon the difficulty in acquiring the correct response as a dominant response.

The term *performance* is a confusing word in motor learning because it has a double meaning. Performance is commonly considered to be goal-centered, purposeful, observable behavior of relatively short duration. The term, however, has the additional meaning of referring to behavior occurring after substantial learning has taken place, and little improvement in responses occurs with additional practice (correct response is dominant). Learning is considered to be a rather permanent change in behavior brought about through practice. In drive theory terms, learning is the process of changing the dominant response from an incorrect response to a correct response.

Thus to test Zajonc's hypothesis, an investigation should compare the performance of individuals practicing alone to those practicing in the presence of an audience when the dominant response is incorrect. Then after sufficient practice, to ensure that the dominant response becomes the correct response, again compare the performance of individuals practicing alone with those practicing in the presence of an audience. Additionally, a physiological indicant to detect changes in arousal level (such as palmar sweating) is essential to determine the accuracy of Zajonc's hypothesis.

A study like this was done by Martens (1969) using a coincident timing motor task and college males as subjects and audience members. The results clearly showed that when learning a complex motor skill (analogous to hitting a baseball), the presence of ten passive spectators impaired the subjects' initial performance as compared to individuals learning alone. On the other hand, after the skill had been reasonably well learned, individuals performing in the presence of an audience were superior to those performing alone. Significant increases in palmar sweating occurred among individuals learning and performing in the presence of an audience as compared to those learning and performing alone, indicating that the presence of others was arousing.

Additional support for Zajonc's hypothesis in an audience situation has been reported by Rosenquist (1972) using a motor task known as rotary pursuit tracking. The only evidence not supporting Zajonc's hypothesis was reported by Singer (1970) using a mirror tracing task. The significance of this study, however, is dubious because of several important methodological deficiencies.

COACTION EFFECT

Early coaction research predominantly used infrahumans as subjects, and centered on the facilitating effects that other members of the same species have on feeding behavior. Studies on a variety of species have consistently shown facilitation. Allport was one of the early leaders in coaction research with humans and his results were consistent with Zajonc's reformulation. Additional support for the coaction effect has come from studies by Ader and Tatum (1963) and Seidman et al. (1957). In Ader and Tatum's study, graduate and medical students failed to learn an electric-shock-avoidance task when working in pairs but quickly learned the task when working alone. In a situation requiring little learning, Seidman et al. (1957) investigated the ability of individuals to endure electric shock when alone or in the presence of another individual also receiving shock. The findings indicated that subjects tolerated much more shock in a group situation than alone.

The ability to endure more pain or to sustain a physical effort is an important part of achieving excellence in sport. Seidman's study suggests that the perceived sharing of stress contributes to stress tolerance. Support for this notion also comes from research by Schachter (1959). Within the professions of physical education and coaching, the question as to whether or not the presence of others experiencing the same physical stress influences another individual's tolerance for it is relevant. This question was tested by Martens and Landers (1969) with boys of three different age groups. The task was to extend one leg horizontally while sitting and to hold it in that position for as long as possible, a task that becomes quite painful in a short period of time. One-third of the subjects within each age group did the task alone, another third in pairs (dyads), and another in groups of four (tetrads). The results clearly showed that the tetrads held their legs in the extended position much longer than the dyads or alone group for all three age groups.

The studies by Seidman et al. (1957) and Martens and Landers (1969) provide evidence that coactors facilitate performance on tasks requiring little learning. This conclusion, which is consistent with Zajonc's hypothesis, is corroborated by Carment and Latchford (1970), who found that coactors increased the rate of responding on a simple motor task. But only the study by Ader and Tatum (1963), using a nonmotor task, provides any evidence that learning is impaired when in the presence of coactors. Thus we need to determine if the presence of coactors impairs the learning of complex motor skills.

Some evidence to answer this question was recently obtained from a study in which college males were tested either alone, in dyads, triads, or tetrads. (Martens and Landers, 1972.) The subjects were required to perform a very difficult and novel motor skill in one of the four coaction situations. The study supported the hypothesis that increasing numbers of coactors result in increasing motor impairment during initial learning. These findings were replicated in an experiment by Burwitz and Newell (1972).

EVALUATION APPREHENSION

So far, evidence has generally supported Zajonc's social facilitation hypothesis, but an adequate explanation as to why it occurs has not been obtained. Zajonc's explanation was that the *mere presence of others* is arousing and arousal enhances the emission of the dominant response. Later research, however, indicates this may be an oversimplification.

Studies by Cottrell et al. (1968), Henchy and Glass (1968), Klinger (1969), and Martens and Landers (1972) have shown that the presence of an audience or coactor who could not evaluate the individual's performance (e.g., blindfolded audience) did not produce the social facilitation phenomenon. Instead, only when the audience was in a position to evaluate the subject's performance did inhibitory or facilitory effects occur. It appears then that the mere presence of others is not a sufficient condition for social facilitation to occur, but the audience or coactors must be perceived as having the potential to evaluate the subject's performance. Why is the potential for evaluation the important ingredient in the presence of others? Because from previous experiences each of us has learned to associate positive or negative outcomes with evaluative situations. When we play a game well we are evaluated favorably and the outcome is positive. When we play poorly the evaluation is unfavorable and the outcome is negative.

Recent evidence has shown that the *form* of evaluation has considerable influence on the potency of the social facilitation phenomenon. In the study by Martens and Landers, college males learned a complex motor skill under one of three conditions: direct evaluation of performance, evaluation of performance outcome (indirect evaluation), and no evaluation. The results supported Cottrell's (1968) notion that the social facilitation phenomenon occurs as a result of a learned response to evaluative situations. The study also showed that direct evaluation (observing the actual performance) produced much stronger effects than indirect evaluation. In the indirect evaluation condition, coactors could only evaluate the *outcome* of the performance and not the performance itself. This finding is not difficult to illustrate in everyday experiences. Typists, for example, often are seriously disrupted by their employer standing over their shoulder, but are not as disrupted when typing unobserved and then presenting the finished product to their employer for evaluation. Similarly, a student in class becomes very unsettled when his teacher observes him doing an assignment at his desk, but is not nearly as apprehensive when doing the assignment alone and later submitting it.

FACTORS MEDIATING THE
SOCIAL FACILITATION PHENOMENON

A variety of variables may determine precisely how the presence of evaluating others affects any particular individual. These factors fall into the categories of individual, situation, and task variables.

Individual Variables

Under this category one variable receiving attention has been the personality disposition of *anxiety*. A study by Cox (1968) found that high anxious children decreased their rate of performance and low anxious children increased their rate of performance when in the presence of others. Cox suggested that the presence of another person was interpreted as transforming the situation into an evaluative one for high anxious children, causing their anxiety to interfere with performance; for low anxious children an observer was assumed to provide an incentive for more efficient performance. Ganzer (1968) found similar results. Observer presence was detrimental for high and moderately anxious females, but not for the low anxious females. Martens (1969), however, found no evidence that a person's anxiety level mediated the audience effect on a motor task. Different anxiety scales, different subject populations, and different tasks may account for the differences in these findings. At any rate, additional research is needed before we can understand how anxiety affects behavior in the presence of others.

Although little direct evidence is available, an important factor related to social facilitation effects is the person's *ability*. Gates (1924) has suggested that more proficient performers are disturbed by the audience and the less proficient are aided, which is somewhat contradictory to Zajonc's hypothesis. Cottrell (1968) found that slow- and medium-speed learners performed consistent with Zajonc's hypothesis, but an audience did not affect the high-speed learners. One additional study concerned with ability was completed by Singer (1965), where he compared athletes and nonathletes performing a balancing task in the presence of an audience. The results showed that nonathletes performed better in the presence of others than the athletes. Although these findings may seem surprising, there is no reason to believe that an athlete with considerable ability in one

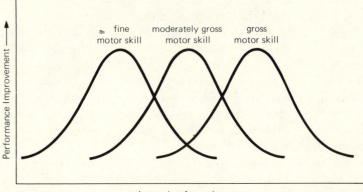

Figure 2.1. The inverted-U curve.

sport should also have high ability in a novel motor skill. But, on the other hand, they should not be expected to perform worse than the nonathletes. Perhaps the athletes perceived themselves as being expected to be superior on such skills; thus when in the presence of an evaluative audience, the athletes were more aroused and hence performed worse than the nonathletes, who had less expectations of themselves in motor activities. Certainly the relationship between ability level and performance in the presence of others warrants further study.

Arousal has been the key variable in explaining social facilitation effects. Another variable that may mediate the effects of an audience is the state of arousal that the person is in when presented with an audience situation. When the dominant response is the correct response, the social facilitation hypothesis predicts that increased arousal from the presence of others facilitates performance. There is some reason to believe that for a well-learned task, continued increases in arousal would not continue to improve performance, ad infinitum. When an individual reaches extremely high levels of arousal, both perceptual and motor processes become disrupted. Therefore it is likely that moderate increases in arousal will facilitate performance on a well-learned task, but continued increases in arousal will disrupt performance. This relationship is known as the inverted-U hypothesis (see Figure 2.1), or the Yerkes-Dodson law, and is among the best known hypotheses in psychology.

The inverted-U hypothesis commonly has been thought to be a well-established relationship and although some evidence does support it, the arousal-performance relationship appears to be considerably more complex than what was initially assumed by this hypothesis. (See Martens, 1972.) As the social facilitation literature reveals, the arousal-performance relationship is affected by whether the dominant response is the correct or incorrect response. Also the person's personality, other situational factors, the task, and the conditions eliciting arousal all appear to affect this relationship.

But to return to our initial concern: How does the presence of others influence the arousal-performance relationship? The available evidence suggests the following hypothesis: A person low in arousal initially should perform according to Zajonc's prediction when moderately aroused by the presence of others. But if the person is in a high arousal state initially, the presence of others increases arousal even more, disrupting performance. Although we have no direct test of this hypothesis, if the inverted-U and social facilitation hypotheses are correct, it is a logical deduction. But again the situation does not appear to be this simple. Some evidence suggests that when a person experiences high levels of arousal, the presence of others may be comforting and actually reduce rather than increase arousal. (Schachter, 1959.) Thus a high arousal state is decreased by the presence of others and a low arousal state is increased by the presence of others. We may then hypothesize that the presence of others has a tendency to maximize performance by shifting arousal to a moderate state. This final supposition, as well as the entire arousal-performance relationship, needs considerable additional experimental attention before we thoroughly understand this relationship.

Task Variables

We have already discussed how task characteristics influence the social facilitation phenomenon in simple and complex terms. The presence of others will facilitate performance on a simple task and impair performance on a complex, unlearned task. Another factor that we need to consider is the relationship between audience- or coactor-elicited arousal and performance on fine and gross motor skills. Oxendine (1970) has indicated, although experimental evidence does not directly confirm, that the level of arousal for optimum performance of a fine motor skill is considerably less than the arousal level for optimum performance on a gross motor skill (see Figure 2.1). According to this hypothesis, if a professional golfer manifested the same arousal state as that of a linebacker in a football game, his performance would suffer. This hypothesis has strong intuitive plausibility, but has little scientific evidence to substantiate it.

Situational Variables

One of the primary interests in this section is the relationship between the characteristics of the audience members or coactors and the performer. For example, does a supportive audience influence a performer differently than a nonsupportive audience? In one study, Kozar (1970) failed to find any differences between these two types of audiences when performing a gross motor balancing task. A number of other situational variables need to be studied, but as yet have not been. For example, what is the influence on a performer when he knows the audience members or coactors? When they are his friends? When they are not his friends? When the audience members have high status? Other variables that must be taken into account are age and sex differences between the performer and the audience. The size of the audience or the number of coactors needs further attention. The formality of the situation may heighten or lessen arousal manifested by the presence of others. And finally, it would be helpful to know how previous experience in the presence of others influences performance.

CONCLUSION

We have seen that what may appear to be a rather simple phenomenon, the effect of the presence of other individuals, is not as simple and straightforward as might be initially expected. Probably the most consistent finding in all of social psychology has been Zajonc's reformulation. The presence of others is detrimental when initially learning both verbal and motor tasks, but facilitates performance of these tasks once they are well learned. Evidence also clearly shows that the mere presence of others is not the prime source for producing social facilitation; instead it is the evaluation apprehension associated with the presence of others who have the potential to evaluate the individual positively or negatively. To the physical educator the implications of this chapter seem fairly obvious. When teaching motor skills, particularly to individuals who become nervous in the presence of others, instruction in nonevaluative situations should be superior to instruction in evaluative situations. Additionally, when wishing to facilitate performance of motor skills that are well learned, the presence of an evaluative audience should help.

CHAPTER 3

IMITATION AND OBSERVATIONAL LEARNING

We have just considered how the presence of other individuals in the form of an audience or coactors influences individual behavior. We shift our focus now and consider how the observation of others performing some act affects an audience of one. In this chapter we will examine two theories that postulate how the process of imitation occurs, and we will then focus our attention on how observing a human model perform some motor skill influences the observer's acquisition of that skill.

Imitation is a general term that describes increased behavior similarity between a model and the observer of the model. One form of imitation, which is our primary concern here, is known as observational learning or vicarious learning. When an individual approximates his behavior to that of a model as a way to learn some behavior, it is known as *observational learning*. Observational learning then is a special kind of learning in which the cues controlling the selection of particular actions in behavior are social rather than impersonal. Of course, imitative behavior that does not reflect learning may occur; that is, the elicited behavior was already available in the observer's behavioral repertoire and the model served only as a stimulus to elicit the previously learned response.

Bandura (1969), one of the leading researchers on imitation, has said, "One of the fundamental means by which new modes of behavior are acquired and existing patterns are modified entails modeling and vicarious processes" (p. 118). And it has been said that the importance of learning by observation is obvious and observable. Actually much learning by observation is avoidance learning. By observing a bicyclist being hit when swerving in front of a car, a child burned by touching a hot stove, or a canoeist crashing into rocks when traversing a series of rapids, we quickly and effectively learn to modify our behavior in these situations without having to directly experience the negative consequences. But observational learning can also be positive learning. Learning by observation is particularly important in the socialization process through which culture is transmitted.

Before we examine imitation and, specifically, observational learning more closely, two cautions are in order. Thus far the impression may have been that imitation is always desirable and is an all-encompassing phenomenon. That indeed is not true. Although imitation is desired in some areas of behavior, it is not in other areas. For example, language skills and basic movement patterns are readily learned by imitation, but imitation does not facilitate creative writing or creative modern dancing. The second point is that even though much verbal and social learning occurs through vicarious processes, the uses of imitation appear limited. A person cannot learn to be a quarterback or a high-speed typist merely by watching others do these activities. This is not to imply, however, that modeling does not serve an important function in the acquisition of quarterbacking or typing skills.

In teaching complex motor skills it is apparent that the learner must somehow be given information about the content of the complex motor response to be learned and then be given an opportunity to practice. The information can be provided in at least two ways: (1) visual cues through demonstration and (2) verbal cues through instruction. Our concern in this chapter is with the function that modeling plays in providing visual cues. Bandura (1969) has noted, however, that verbal cues, when associated with visual images, are simply symbolic mediators for visual images. That is, I might ask you to do a full turn of the body on the tip of the toe of your right foot. This description serves as a verbal model informing you of the movement requested. I could abbreviate this verbal description by asking you to do a pirouette, which would elicit a certain movement assuming you knew the meaning of pirouette.

In teaching motor skills we usually say "do it this way," or "watch me," or "like this," and then proceed to demonstrate the skill. Physical educators appear to rely more on visual cues through demonstration than on verbal cues as a means of presenting the desired movement. Why is this? More than likely it is because visual cues are more precise than verbal cues; that is, our nomenclature to describe human movement is inarticulate and undeveloped. And it is also because visual cues convey information more rapidly.

For complex movements then, modeling is an expedient way to inform the learner what is to be practiced; to help him form a plan of what to do. But practice is not always essential for learning. For simple motor responses perhaps only one demonstration is sufficient for immediate correct performance. For complex tasks, however, the need for practice as a supplement to modeling becomes essential for learning to occur. (Sheffield, 1961.)

Because of the reliance upon observational learning by physical educators and coaches, it is somewhat an enigma that people in these professions know so little about observational learning, and that they commonly ignore it in professional preparation. Although it is obvious that we learn by observing others, many aspects of observational learning remain obscure as they pertain to motor skill acquisition. For example:

1. How effective are teachers versus student peers as models for facilitating the learning of motor skills?
2. How much time should be spent modeling and how much time practicing?
3. Should the entire skill be modeled as a whole or in segments?
4. Do characteristics of the model (e.g., age, status, sex, personality) influence the learning by the observers?
5. Does reinforcing the observer for the correct imitation of a modeled act facilitate additional imitative behavior?
6. Does reinforcing the model (known as vicarious reinforcement) and not the observer facilitate the learning of motor skills?
7. Does observing a film of a proficient athlete performing a complex sport skill actually transmit information or is the film more of a motivational tool?
8. What types of skills are learned more readily through observation and what types of skills are not?

Unfortunately we have very little experimental evidence to answer these questions scientifically. Physical educators and coaches, however, must answer these questions in part every day by their decision whether to use modeling procedures. Exactly what guides the teacher in using modeling procedures? The answer probably is reflected in the old adage, "We teach as we were taught," and thus "We model as we observed." Somewhat reluctantly then we leave the security of the scientific method to venture upon speculative territory because we hope to shed some light on this important topic. To do so we will examine the current research and conceptual status of imitation and observational learning in social psychology as directed toward verbal and social behavior, suggesting implications for motor behavior when possible.

HOW OBSERVATIONAL LEARNING OCCURS
In 1903 Tarde identified what he believed to be the only important social processes—invention and imitation. According to Tarde, imitation was the most important process because

if inventions or innovations are not imitated, they have no enduring social value. Indeed at the turn of the century, because imitation was so readily observable in animals and man, it was considered to be an instinct. When instinct psychology justifiably fell into disrepute, imitation fell with it.

Later, in attempting to excavate imitation from the instinct doctrine, Miller and Dollard (1941) were able to rekindle interest in this phenomenon by showing that one form of imitation could be controlled by instrumental conditioning procedures and not instinct. Although Miller and Dollard's initial formulation of instrumental learning constructs to explain imitative behavior encountered much criticism, it paved the way for subsequent social learning theories of imitation. Two theories are particularly prominent: the generalized imitation theory of Gewirtz and Stingle (1968) and Bandura's contiguity-mediational theory. These theories differ sharply on how new responses are initially acquired by observing a model.

Like Miller and Dollard, Gewirtz and Stingle (1968) use basic instrumental conditioning and S-R chaining concepts to explain the development of generalized imitation. For the young child the development of generalized imitation involves:

1. An imitative response occurring by chance or through direct training (shaping procedures) or direct physical assistance;
2. When the response occurs it is strengthened and maintained by extrinsic reinforcement; and
3. After several imitative responses are established, a class of diverse but functionally equivalent behaviors is acquired and maintained by intermittent extrinsic reinforcement.

Gewirtz and Stingle emphasize that extrinsic reinforcement is essential in *learning to imitate* and hence in developing generalized imitation, although once developed, extrinsic reinforcement is not always essential. Thus these authors define generalized imitation as occurring "when many different responses of a model are copied in diverse situations often in the absence of extrinsic reinforcement" (p. 375).

To understand the generalized imitation theory, it is important to recognize the distinction between *learning to imitate* and *learning by imitation*. Learning to imitate follows procedures identical to those described by Miller and Dollard for matched-dependent learning. That is, imitative learning occurs when a model responds to a stimulus and the model's response serves as a new stimulus for an observer's response. If this event is reinforced the observer learns the connection between the model's response and his own response. In the young child during the early years of socialization, the opportunities for learning to imitate are numerous. Evidence has shown that as the child learns to imitate diverse responses and is reinforced for matching responses, these behaviors generalize to new situations, new behaviors, and new models. In contrast, learning by imitation occurs only when the stimulus initially responded to by the model is a discriminable stimulus for the observer, and the observer connects his response to this initial stimulus as well as the model's response to it. The more diverse the stimulus-response links the more learning by imitation. *However, before a person can learn by imitation he must learn to imitate.* Thus Gewirtz and Stingle theorize that through the development of generalized imitation, which follows basic instrumental conditioning procedures, individuals learn to imitate and subsequently learn by imitation.

The contiguity-mediational theory formulated by Bandura (1969) differs from Gewirtz and Stingle's position primarily on how novel responses are learned by imitation. The contiguity-mediational theory postulates that sensory images aroused by the modeling stimuli become structured perceptual responses through association by contiguity (adjacent in time). For example, throwing a baseball overhand with the right arm requires a series of movements involving various parts of the body. Observations of these various movements are associated by the fact that certain segments precede and follow other segments temporally. This association of contiguous stimuli occurs either through *perceptual* or *symbolic* mediators or both; these then serve as guides for the later reproduction of matching responses. Both mediators refer to how the brain codes the information received from the model. Perceptual mediators refer to the imaginal representational system (analogous to a video recorder) and the symbolic mediators refer to the verbal representational system (analogous to an audio recorder). That is, modeling stimuli are coded into images or words for memory representation and then they function as mediators for subsequent response retrieval and reproduction. Some evidence to support Bandura's contiguity-mediational theory has been obtained. (E.g., Bandura et al., 1966; Gerst, 1971.)

Whether or not observational learning actually occurs, according to Bandura, is a function of the following components:

1. Attention processes that regulate sensory registration of modeling stimuli;
2. Retention processes that are influenced by mental rehearsal operations and symbolic coding of modeled events into easily remembered schemes;
3. Motoric reproduction processes that are concerned with the availability of component responses and the use of symbolic codes in guiding behavioral reproduction;
4. Incentive or motivational processes that determine whether or not acquired responses will be activated into overt performances.

Thus Bandura distinguishes between processes that influence the learning of a response (the first two components) and the processes that influence the actual performance of the learned response (the latter two components). According to Bandura's theory, the acquisition of imitative behaviors is seen as a function of the observer simply being exposed to a model's response independent of any reinforcement. The actual performance of a learned response, however, depends heavily on reinforcement contingencies.

Evidence tends to support premises from both Gewirtz and Stingle's theory and Bandura's theory and the issue is not close to a resolution. Below we examine in greater detail the four components outlined by Bandura because they are useful in organizing the existing literature and in further discussing observational learning of motor skills.

Attention Processes
It almost goes without saying that for observational learning to occur the observer must attend to the modeled response. But

to how much can he attend. In most complex motor skills many movements occur rapidly and simultaneously. Can the observer attend to all of the features of an outstanding tennis pro serving the ball? It appears unlikely. Thus the presentation of a modeled act must take into consideration whether or not information is conveyed and how much of this information is absorbed or perceived. Several possible methods may be used to help ensure that information is conveyed and perceived. Slow-motion filming would appear to be useful, except perhaps in motor skills that emphasize timing. Another possible procedure for resolving the information overload problem is the use of verbal guidance or cues. Guiding the observer's attention should facilitate his selection of the most critical information bits in the modeled response. It is also possible that verbal guidance assists the observer in developing a symbolic representation of the modeled event. Thus we should expect that complex motor skills that are presented both visually and verbally are acquired more readily than items that are presented through only one modality.

Closely associated with the information overload problem is the concern about the discriminability of modeling stimuli and its effect on motor skill acquisition. Bandura (1969) notes that "modeled characteristics that are highly discernible can be more readily acquired than subtle attributes which must be abstracted from heterogeneous responses differing on numerous stimulus dimensions" (p. 138). The poor discriminability of many complex motor skills modeled in films used in physical education instruction makes it highly unlikely that they facilitate skill acquisition beyond providing an indication of the primary objective of the task. For example, it is improbable that an observer can absorb all of the information presented in a 20-minute film illustrating all the strokes in tennis. Nor are some of the stimuli necessary for correct performance discernible in such a skill. Some films, however, are much better than others. In some films an effort has been made to discriminate the critical features of a complex motor skill by using verbal cues and by focusing the camera on a particular aspect of the modeled performance.

Rentention Processes

The second component of observational learning is retention. It is obvious that the original observational inputs must be retained in some form if learning is to occur. Bandura's theory postulates that this information is stored in imaginal forms and symbolic codes. Based on previous retention research, it seems probable that the retention of a modeled motor skill is facilitated by symbolic coding. (Gerst, 1971.) Overt practice should also provide an opportunity for the observer to code and organize the patterns of behavior into integrated units. Although we will discuss overt practice later, Bandura (1969) has suggested that covert rehearsal may also facilitate retention of observed behavior.

Covert practice, or mental practice as it usually is called in physical education, has been beneficial when learning some motor skills. Sheffield (1961) concluded from his research that covert practice is more efficient because it is more rapid, contains fewer actual steps, and is less subject to interference than overt practice. Although some research has shown that covert practice facilitates the learning of motor skills, an equal amount of evidence has not documented any improvement. The inconsistencies in the effectiveness of covert practice are not explainable. One likely factor, however, is that some motor responses are not easily translated into perceptual sequences. Experimental evidence by Corbin (1967) suggests that previous overt practice on the motor task may facilitate the ease with which imaginal or symbolic coding takes place. Thus we may expect that covert practice has a greater probability of facilitating motor skill acquisition when it is easily represented as a perceptual sequence or has been practiced previously. Covert rehearsal may also be very effective in tasks requiring high degrees of symbolic coding, a characteristic unfamiliar to many motor tasks.

Retention decrements occur primarily from interference. Interference arising from material learned previous to the observational input is known as proactive inhibition; interference arising from material succeeding observational input is known as retroactive inhibition. Massed exposure of numerous stimuli creates substantial interference and may confuse the learner.

Retention is greater when modeled cues are presented in smaller units and at spaced intervals. A final important factor influencing the retention of an observed performance is the motivational state of the observer and the consequences arising from the modeled performance. We shall leave this concern for later consideration when discussing incentives.

Motor Reproduction Processes

From our own experience we know that it is difficult if not impossible to accurately reproduce a complex motor response without having previously practiced the skill. Many complex motor skills, however, are really only a series of simpler components or subunits. The learning of motor skills by observation occurs most easily when the skills require the synthesis of previously acquired components. In this situation, learning is probably most efficient if the task is broken down into its constituent parts and each is acquired separately before the whole pattern is attempted. Sheffield (1961) refers to these constituent parts as natural or inherent subunits of the task and he has shown that learning is more efficient on perceptual-discrimination tasks when so divided. Bandura, discussing the motor reproduction process, states:

> The problem of behavioral reproduction is further complicated in the case of highly coordinated motor skills, such as golf, in which a person cannot observe many of the responses he is making and must therefore primarily rely upon proprioceptive feedback cues. For these reasons, performances that contain many motor factors usually require, in addition to the guidance of a proficient model, some overt practice. [1969:142.]

Based on the contiguity-mediational theory of observational learning and basic learning theory, a good strategy for the acquisition of complex motor skills would appear to be:

1. Model the entire motor response;
2. Model the first natural subunit;

3. Practice the first natural subunit until acquired;
4. Repeat steps 2 and 3 for each succeeding subunit;
5. Repeat step 1, modeling the integration of the subunits;
6. Practice the integration of the subunits.

If many subunits were involved, the integration of subunits in steps 5 and 6 may have to be done gradually, building on previously learned subunits. This procedure, of course, is not uncommon in instruction of motor skills. Known as the whole-part-whole method of learning, it is supported by observational learning research. (Sheffield, 1961.)

An obvious limitation to the acquisition of a motor skill is that although the modeled response may be attended to and retained in representational form, because of physical limitations it cannot be reproduced. Not all persons have the inherent ability to learn all complex motor skills to a high level of proficiency. For example, a person may be too short, obese, or blind, or he may not have the incentive to learn or perform a learned skill. The incentive problem is considered next.

Incentives
Attention, retention, and the actual motor reproduction of modeled behavior are all affected by the fourth component, the motivational or incentive variable. Having attended to a modeled performance, having retained it, and having the capability to perform the modeled behavior will *not* lead to observational learning if positive incentives do not motivate the observer to behave accordingly.

In an observational learning sequence a *training period* occurs where the observer watches the model; this is followed by a *testing period* where the observer performs. To date, the prime motivational variable studied in imitation experiments has been reinforcement, primarily social reinforcement. Flanders (1968) has developed a classification scheme for distinguishing reinforcement conditions during training from reinforcement conditions during testing. This scheme is useful when reviewing the experimental evidence concerned with incentives and modeling.

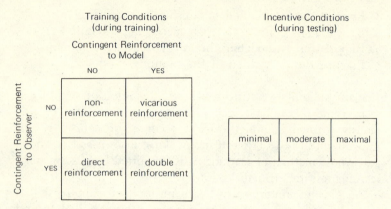

Figure 3.1. Flanders' models for classifying reinforcement conditions during training and for testing for observational learning.

Figure 3.1 illustrates this scheme. During training, the four reinforcement conditions are determined by the presence or absence of reinforcement to the observer and model. During testing, Flanders describes three positive incentive conditions that are based solely on rewards to the observer. Presumably only positive incentive would result in observational learning.

What are the effects of direct and vicarious reinforcement on imitative behavior during the training behavior? Based on the evidence reviewed by Flanders (1968), a partial reward to the observer increases imitation when the reward is contingent upon the imitative response. Partial reinforcement, however, decreases imitation when the reward is contingent upon task-success and not imitation. Partially reinforced imitative responses seem to be more resistant to extinction than continuously reinforced imitative responses.

The experimental evidence supports the generalization that reinforcement to the model during training or vicarious reinforcement increases imitation of the model by the observer. The implication of this finding is that observers more frequently imitate successful models. Moreover, the more frequently a model's responses are rewarded, the more the observer tends to imitate those responses. Additionally it has been found that nonreinforcement training conditions have been sufficient for acquiring at least some imitative behaviors.

With regard to the effects of incentives on the actual performance of observed behavior, evidence indicates that maximal incentive conditions tend to elicit more imitation than minimal or moderate incentive conditions. Also, characteristics of the model may function as motivational factors influencing an observer's imitative behavior. For example, observers more readily imitate models of higher status. Evidence also supports the position that observers imitate models who control resources valued by the observer. Despite a possibility that the effects of live models may be more enduring, the tremendous impact of filmed or televised exposure compared to live performances is apparent.

The effects of antecedent characteristics of the observer must also be considered. Flanders (1968) notes that the most consistent finding is that boys imitate aggressive behavior more than girls. Also it has been shown that higher levels of physiological arousal in an observer can increase imitation up to a point, whereafter further increases in arousal decrease imitation. Currently, an active area of research is in determining the generalizability of imitative behavior; that is, how similar must the observer's task and the model's task be for observational learning to occur?

THE MODEL'S BEHAVIOR

From Chapter 2 we learned that the presence of others energizes behavior (social facilitation), and in this chapter we learned that the presence of others influences the direction of behavior (observational learning). In certain situations then, particularly coaction situations, a person may both energize behavior and, as a model, direct behavior. Thus we need to understand the relative contributions of both modeling and social facilitation on human behavior.

Although done with rats, some insight into the relationship between social facilitation and modeling effects is obtained from a study by Zentall and Levine (1972). In a coaction situation, learning was facilitated when observing a coactor who correctly modeled the responses to be learned; the more correct responses modeled, the more learning improved. Observing coactors emit incorrect responses, however, retarded learning, as compared to rats learning alone. Although we cannot generalize these findings to humans, they suggest an important modification of Zajonc's social facilitation hypothesis, which is important in human learning. Namely, it suggests that the presence of others in a coaction situation facilitates learning when coactors model correct responses, but impairs learning when incorrect cues are modeled. Moreover, these incorrect responses are a greater impairment to the learner than if he were simply allowed to practice alone.

To say it another way, Zentall and Levine's study suggests: Model correctly or do not model at all. And normally we assume that modeling correctly is pedagogically sound. But is it always? Is any information obtained from watching incorrect performances? Is the discriminability of modeled stimuli increased not only by observing a model perform correctly, but by modeling the entire learning sequence beginning initially with incorrect performances and gradually modeling more correctly? Two experiments (Martens et al., 1973) investigated these questions using filmed models. In the first experiment a relatively easy task was used, which required rolling a ball up an inclined board to a target area. In the second experiment the task was much more difficult, requiring a person to move a ball between two rods by manipulating the distance between the rods. In both experiments subjects watched one of four films depicting (1) only correct performances, (2) only incorrect performances, (3) a learning sequence (incorrect performances changing to correct performances), or (4) a control film irrelevant to the tasks.

The results of these experiments showed that for the simple task, none of the modeling films affected performance differently. With the complex task, a particular strategy was necessary to perform well. The results showed that this strategy was modeled when observing both the correct and the learning sequence films. The results did not show, however, that the learning sequence film was superior to the correct performance model.

Additional evidence regarding the relationship between the quality of a model's behavior and the quality of an observer's behavior is obtained from a study by Harney and Landers (1973). This study investigated the influence of observing a skillful or unskillful performance by a model who was either a teacher or a peer of the subject. The results for the teachers are consistent with the findings of Zentall and Levine (1972); that is, subjects who observed a skilled teacher model performed substantially better than subjects who observed an unskilled teacher model. This study, however, also reported the unexplainable finding that observing an unskilled peer model facilitated performance more than observing a skilled peer model.

SOME FINAL QUESTIONS

Recall that in teaching all motor skills we initially model the skill through demonstration or describe it with verbal instructions. Of interest to physical educators is knowing whether or not additional demonstration facilitates the rate of improvement once the initial task objectives are known by the student; that is, does additional modeling facilitate learning more than trial-and-error practice? On a multiple-choice maze task the answer is yes. Studies have shown superior performances by college students (Hillix and Marx, 1960; Rosenbaum and Schutz, 1967) and grade school children (Rosenbaum, 1967) when learning with modeling procedures as compared to trial-and-error practice only. It is likely, however, that the complete answer to this question depends upon the characteristics of the task.

Therefore an important related question is: In what types of motor skills is learning most likely to be facilitated by modeling? Actually most of this chapter has been indirectly concerned with answering this question. Throughout this chapter emphasis has been placed upon modeling as a means of conveying information to the observer about how to do the skill. Modeling, then, helps the observer form a plan for making his motor response. Skills that have complex or difficult responses ordinarily require more complex motor plans, and thus should benefit more from modeling than tasks that have simple motor plans. Sheffield (1961) reports some support for this supposition. He found that the tasks in which demonstration was most beneficial were complex motor tasks requiring a series of sequentially performed motor responses. Familiar examples of such tasks include a gymnastics routine, a dance step, and a take-down in wrestling.

In what types of motor skills is learning facilitated by modeling? Although we cannot further answer this question now, clearly it is among the more important questions that physical education research needs to answer in the coming years.

Another popular question asked by physical educators is: Does observing commercially prepared films of sport skills facilitate the learning of these skills? Based upon the frequent use of these visual aids, the expectation would be that their value has been clearly established. Moreover it might be thought that the production of these visual aids is based on considerable research, with particular concern for producing films that maximize attention and retention. Unfortunately the scientific basis for the production and use of commercially prepared sport skill films is nil.

CONCLUSION

We have attempted to review some conceptual and experimental work in a currently popular area of social psychology. In some cases we have made direct hypotheses about the influence of modeling on motor behavior, in others we have left this task to you. The void in good research on this most important phenomenon has necessitated this strategy. Within the near future, however, it is likely that more research on observational learning will be done by physical educators. Before leaving the area of observational learning, attention must be drawn to one final point. Although our emphasis in this chapter has been on motor skill acquisition, physical educators and coaches are potentially important models for the learning of both verbal and social skills. We shall consider the role of modeling in learning social skills in Part III.

CHAPTER 4

SOCIAL REINFORCEMENT

Physical educators, coaches, and others teaching motor skills often provide students with information or feedback at the end of an instructional interchange. This feedback may serve one or more of the following purposes: (1) to provide information as to whether the response was correct or incorrect; (2) to change the person's motivational state; and (3) as a reinforcer to change the respondent's behavior in a desired direction. This feedback may be presented in a variety of ways. One general form of feedback is known as knowledge of results and a second type is social reinforcement. In this chapter we will acquaint ourselves with the reinforcement language, look spe-

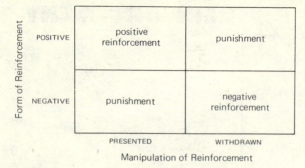

Figure 4.1.   Reinforcement nomenclature.

cifically at social reinforcement as it influences behavior, and finally, examine the role of social reinforcement in motor learning and performance.

To this point then, we have discussed how behavior may be energized or aroused by the presence of others and how it may be directed by observing a model. In this chapter we will learn that social reinforcement may both energize and direct behavior. This chapter will be considerably more meaningful to the student who has some introduction to the psychology of learning. For the student with little background in this area, it will be helpful to read an introductory text such as Travers' *Essentials of Learning* (1972).

REINFORCEMENT TERMINOLOGY

The reinforcement language is somewhat confusing because we often do not use precise nomenclature when referring to various forms of reinforcement. *Reinforcement* is actually a neutral term referring to one of the operations that will increase the strength of a response. A *positive reinforcer* is any stimulus which, when it follows a response, will increase the strength or maintain the occurrence of that response. A *negative reinforcer* is a stimulus, the removal of which increases the strength of a response. Negative reinforcement is a term that is seldom used correctly. Instead we often think of negative reinforcement as being any aversive stimulus. By considering whether the reinforcer was positive or negative and whether the reinforcer was presented or withdrawn, we may distinguish two classes of reward and two classes of punishment.

From Figure 4.1 we can see that:

1. If a positive reinforcer is presented to an organism following a response, the result is positive reinforcement or positive *reward*.
2. If a positive reinforcer is withdrawn following an organism's response, the result is negative *punishment*.
3. If a negative reinforcer is presented to an organism following a response, the result is positive *punishment*.
4. If a negative reinforcer is withdrawn following an organism's response, the result is negative reinforcement or negative *reward*.

These distinctions may be somewhat confusing, because the terms have been used incorrectly so frequently. In common usage both classes of rewards are referred to as positive reinforcements (1 and 4) and both classes of punishment are called negative reinforcers (2 and 3).

We may briefly illustrate these forms of reinforcement by examining a typical athletic situation. For example, the coach praises you for a fine performance after having played a good game. This is positive reinforcement. During the season you continue to have one fine game after another and each time your coach praises you accordingly. But after one game, although you had played well, the coach failed to praise you. You had learned to expect the praise but now it was withheld—the result is negative punishment. The last game of the season you play disastrously. Now the coach "chews you out" for your inadequate performance. This reproof is positive punishment. Imagine for a moment that your entire season had been a disaster and invariably after each game the coach was derogatory about your play. But now, after the last game of the season, although you played somewhat better, the coach does not praise you, but at least he does not say anything derogatory. The removal of these offensive remarks is an example of negative reward.

Incentive is another term that is frequently used in discussing reinforcement. Incentive refers to the expectation that a reward or punishment will follow a response based on previous experiences in which rewards or punishments were associated with the same response. (Logan and Wagner, 1965.) More commonly, incentive is used erroneously to refer to the reward itself or to the goal. This is somewhat inaccurate because incentive should be limited to the learning process in which the person associates certain rewards and punishments with certain responses, not to the goal itself.

Walker (1967) has described three classes of learning, of which we shall focus on the third: (1) learning of facts, (2) transfer of responses, and (3) learning of skills. As there are several classes of learning, similarly there are many forms of reinforcement. Besides reinforcements being positive or negative, they can be tangible and intangible, intrinsic and extrinsic, social and nonsocial. Our concern, of course, shall be only with social reinforcement, which has been defined as reinforcements under the control of others. This definition is broad and includes many everyday reinforcements. We shall use the term *social reinforcement* in a more limited sense, referring only to non-tangible reinforcement under the control of others. Specifically, verbal and nonverbal communications from one individual to another that increase the strength of a response may be labeled social reinforcements. Praise and reproof, smiles and sneers, friendly and hostile gestures are forms that these social reinforcements frequently take.

Although we do not give attention to the important nonsocial reinforcements, their importance should be recognized. In skill learning, for example, considerable intrinsic feedback is commonly available through the senses in the form of proprioceptive or kinesthetic feedback. Similar extrinsic feedback in the form of knowledge of results is available. Both intrinsic and extrinsic forms of feedback may act as powerful reinforcers. Then, too, there are many tangible things, such as money and food, which are known to be effective reinforcers.

SOCIAL REINFORCEMENT AND
VERBAL AND SOCIAL BEHAVIOR

To better understand the complexity of social reinforcement it is helpful to examine what we have learned about its influence on verbal and social behavior. Little experimental interest was shown in social reinforcement prior to 1958, but since then it has been an active research area, with the major emphasis on how social reinforcement influences verbal and social behavior of children. From this surge of research two conclusions can be safely drawn: (1) there is little doubt that social reinforcement is a potent modifier of behavior, and (2) a number of factors mediate the influence of social reinforcement.

The first conclusion comes as no surprise. Our own daily experiences reinforce the effectiveness that a praise or reproof can have when given by the right person at the right time. The potency of social reinforcement is also corroborated by the success, and hence popularity, of a technique called behavior modification. This technique relies largely on the use of social reinforcement and modeling to change behavior.

To understand the use of social reinforcement more thoroughly, we must give attention to the second conclusion and consider the many factors that mediate the effect of social reinforcement. One of the most consistent findings in the social reinforcement literature has been the cross-sex effect; the finding that female reinforcers have more influence on male recipients and vice versa. (Gewirtz, 1954; Gewirtz and Baer, 1958.) This is not the case, however, with children under five. Both boys and girls in this young age group are most influenced by female reinforcers (Stevenson, 1961). More than likely this is attributable to the matriarchal role in child rearing.

Another interesting difference is that younger children are more affected by social reinforcement than older children. Also, more intelligent children are more affected by social reinforcement. When studying the effectiveness of social reinforcement among middle- and lower-class children, results showed that praise was less effective with middle-class children than with lower-class children. Another finding that many parents may confirm is that unfamiliar adults are more effective reinforcers than familiar adults. Finally, some evidence indicates that praise from a disliked peer is more effective on a child's behavior than praise by a liked peer. Several excellent reviews are available that give a more thorough treatment of these findings. (E.g., Stevenson, 1965; Wodtke and Brown, 1967.)

A number of explanations have been proposed for these findings, but as yet no clear evidence is available to explain *why* these differences occur. The inability to explain why younger children are more affected by social reinforcement than older children, and the like, aptly illustrates the major weakness of social reinforcement research; that is, a lack of theory. Through the 1960s social reinforcement research exemplified the social empiricism approach. More recent work, however, indicates that this area is beginning to adopt the social analysis approach.

One variable that perhaps has stimulated the greatest interest in social reinforcement has been social deprivation. Based on the initial study by Gewirtz and Baer (1958), and subsequently supported several times, it is clear that the potency of social stimuli as reinforcers is increased following social isolation. While Gewirtz and Baer attributed the increase to social deprivation, other writers have offered alternative interpretations, and this phase of social reinforcement research remains active today.

Experimental work on social deprivation has been concerned only with short-term deprivation. It would be informative to know the effectiveness of social reinforcement among individuals who have experienced wide variations in positive and negative social reinforcement throughout their life. That is, how effective are both positive and negative social reinforcements as a function of a person's social reinforcement history? Baron (1966) has recently investigated this question. He observed that each person has an expected standard of social reinforcement, and when social reinforcement is substantially above or below this standard, negative effect or dissonance is produced. For example, after having completed a task successfully, we usually expect to be praised. But if in fact no positive reinforcement is received we begin to wonder why. On the other hand, if someone praises us much more than we expect, we also wonder about his intentions. When social reinforcement is considerably above or below a person's expectation, Baron found that the individual will vary his task performance in a direction that is likely to result in him receiving reinforcement more in line with his expectations. That is, if you expect a moderate amount of positive reinforcement but instead you receive an overabundance of praise, you may attempt to perform less well in order to receive reinforcements more congruent with your expectation. We will refer to this issue again later in this chapter.

Personality dispositions are another group of factors that are thought to mediate the influence of social reinforcement. The major personality variable of experimental interest has been internal-external control of reinforcement, sometimes known as locus of control. As a personality variable, internal control refers to individuals who have a strong expectancy toward "the perception of positive and/or negative events as being a consequence of one's own actions and thereby under personal control." External control refers to individuals characterized as having a strong expectancy toward "the perception of positive and/or negative events as being unrelated to one's own behaviors in certain situations and therefore beyond personal control." (Lefcourt, 1966: 207.) Thus when reinforcement is seen as not contingent upon an individual's own behavior (external control), the influence of social reinforcement should be less than when the reinforcement appears contingent upon his behavior (internal control). Substantial evidence has supported this notion for verbal and social behavior. (Lefcourt, 1966; Rotter, 1966.)

A final issue of considerable interest is the use of social rewards versus the use of social punishments. This is a very old issue and our experimental evidence provides us with little help. To examine this issue we must raise two questions. What is the most effective way to bring about the behavioral change desired —the short-term consideration? And what are the cumulative effects of social rewards and social punishments—the long-term consideration?

Existing evidence attempts to answer only the first and more simple question. These studies have been concerned with the influence of praise and reproof on learning a specific task. The results indicate that the use of punishments alone tends to be a more effective short-term reinforcer than rewards. (Brackbill and O'Hara, 1958; Curry, 1960; Meyer and Seidman, 1960, 1961.) In most of these studies, however, the tasks have involved problems where only one right and one wrong response was possible. Some recent indications are that rewards are more effective than punishments when more than two responses are possible. This is an important distinction because most of the skills we are interested in teaching (including motor skills) are complex and have more than two alternative responses.

Another important point in discussing the effectiveness of rewards and punishments is how a person interprets silence. Crandall et al. (1962) have shown that children interpret an adult's silence as meaning the opposite of the dominant preceding reinforcement. Thus silence is interpreted as approval when preceded by verbal criticism, and is considered disapproval when preceded by verbal praise.

When considering the long-term use of positive or negative social reinforcement there are no clear answers. We might expect that frequent use of social punishments over a long period of time would result in a person losing motivation or withdrawing from the situation. Constant criticism and disapproval probably affects personality adversely, is dissatisfying, and discouraging. Thus the use of social rewards appears to be more advantageous. Using only social rewards, however, has not proved to be very effective either. Perhaps this is so because social rewards tend to satiate the individual and may be incongruent with his reinforcement history. As so often occurs with human behavior it is not either or, but our answer probably lies in the use of a ratio between rewards and punishments, with the ratio somewhat in favor of rewards.

WHY DO SOCIAL
REINFORCERS MODIFY BEHAVIOR?

The various explanations of how social reinforcers modify behavior may be categorized into one of three positions. The first is that social reinforcers energize or motivate behavior primarily by acquiring incentive value. The second position is that social reinforcers act as cues, thus providing information about the appropriateness of a response. The third position, espoused predominantly by Skinner and his followers, is in a sense no position at all. They hold that no explanation is necessary, that the important thing is to determine what stimuli elicit and control what behaviors. They do not attempt to theorize how these processes occur. While many people share Skinner's view, many also reject it as being too superficial. Thus, in the next section, we will examine the influence of social reinforcers on motor behavior from both an information and motivational position.

SOCIAL REINFORCEMENT
AND MOTOR BEHAVIOR

Both experientially, and now experimentally, we have witnessed how social reinforcers influence social and verbal behavior. The experimental evidence also has shown that social reinforcers are effective in modifying behavior on very simple motor tasks; for example, marble dropping, card sorting, and letter cancellation. Both positive and negative social reinforcers have been shown to facilitate performance on these tasks, but positive social reinforcers have longer or more enduring facilitory effects. Most of the findings for verbal and social behavior also hold true for these simple motor responses. But how do social reinforcers facilitate the performance of these simple motor responses? Is it primarily through information conveyed or is it primarily motivational?

The answer appears to be that it is motivational. These simple motor tasks require little if any learning on the part of the children tested because the motor processes necessary for performance were acquired early in life. If learning is unnecessary then information about the response is not useful or necessary to modify the response. Thus a modification in the rate of responding to these tasks is not due to the informational value of the social reinforcement, but, more likely, to the motivational or incentive value. Social reinforcement appears then, to energize behavior in facilitating performance on these simple tasks.

Although an understanding of the influence of social reinforcement on simple motor responses is important, physical educators are much more concerned with facilitating students' acquisition and performance of complex motor skills. Hence our attention now is directed toward the role of social reinforcement in the acquisition of complex motor responses. It should be noted that we cannot give a precise definition to distinguish between simple and complex motor responses in this context, but in comparison to card sorting and marble dropping, skills such as balancing on a stabilometer, throwing a baseball, and shooting a basketball through a hoop are indeed complex.

Two essential features underlie the successful use of social reinforcement: (1) the need for powerful reinforcers and (2) that the reinforcing event be made contingent upon the desired behavior. To determine whether a reinforcer is powerful, we can only examine the effect of a particular social stimulus on some motor response and determine if it was modified. We do know, of course, that some reinforcers have been traditionally shown to be strong modifiers of behavior; for example, money, praise, affection. With respect to the second feature, a reinforcing event can be made contingent in several ways. A social reinforcer can be presented or withdrawn when the behavior occurs or does not occur. Or both positive and negative reinforcement can be presented or withdrawn based on variations in performance. And finally, social reinforcers can be given in various degrees contingent on the response. Thus reinforcers may be given only on trials in which the response meets the reinforcement criteria, or on every trial contingent on the quality of the response. However, a number of studies concerned with motor behavior have used a variety of social stimuli to modify behavior with noncontingent procedures. These studies are using social stimuli solely as *incentives* and not as potential social reinforcers.

Many of the studies using social incentives as independent variables have had methodological weaknesses that make it difficult to render any clear interpretation or reach any generalizations about their findings. The primary social variables examined have been smiles, praise, reproof, attention, and the presence of small groups. As is true in other areas of research, but particularly here, only those studies obtaining significant effects tend to be published, with an unknown number of studies finding nonsignificant effects that do not appear in the literature. With this caution in mind, the only generalization that appears warranted is that some studies have found moderate facilitation for running and endurance tasks, but for complex motor skills, both impairment and facilitation have been reported. Unpublished thesis research, however, suggests that more frequently than not, no effects are found. It is virtually impossible to draw any further inferences from these studies because of their atheoretical conception and diverse methodology.

The research investigating the influence of social stimuli should not be confused with the research studying the influence of social reinforcement because the former studies do not administer positive or negative social rewards or punishments contingent upon the desired behavior to be learned. When social stimuli are administered noncontingently they convey no information about the appropriateness of the response. Thus the noncontingent presentation of social stimuli can only have potential incentive value if in fact the social stimuli are powerful.

Additionally it should be recognized that repeated administration of either praise or reproof on every trial of a performance is more than likely very unrealistic and probably not in accord with one's social reinforcement history. Repeated overevaluation and underevaluation of an individual's performance level is sometimes used by instructors as a motivational technique. This false feedback, if used repeatedly, may give an individual an inaccurate perception of his performance ability. Just what this may do to his subsequent motor performance has not been investigated. Interestingly, Aronson and Carlsmith (1962) and others have shown that a motive is operative in individuals to confirm their performance expectancy, be it positive or negative. Thus it is possible, for example, that although criticism and reproof may improve immediate performance, over time such criticism may develop a very low performance expectancy that the individual will subsequently attempt to confirm. An individual's performance expectancy, in conjunction with his social reinforcement history and its influence on his actual motor performance, needs experimental attention.

We now direct our attention to those studies that have investigated the influence of social stimuli administered contingently on complex motor skill acquisition and performance. Although additional evidence is available, a series of studies by the author and his colleagues will serve to illustrate the general findings. In these studies reinforcement was administered on the basis of a schedule, which for the positive social reinforcement groups consisted of praise and smiles when a performance improved over a previous trial, but consisted of nothing when performance did not improve. The subjects in the negative social reinforcement group received reproof and sneers when their performance deteriorated over a previous trial. Sometimes a combined positive and negative group was used. Subjects were always required to learn a motor task that was novel and difficult enough so that substantial learning was required.

In the initial study (Martens, 1970), preschool boys and girls were to learn a ball-rolling task. One group of boys and girls received only positive social reinforcement, another only negative social reinforcement, and another both positive and negative social reinforcement, all administered contingently. In addition to a control group that received no comments, a second control group engaged in conversation with the experimenter, but the experimenter provided no indication of performance evaluation. The results failed to show any significant differences between any of the five conditions. From this initial study we conjectured that no differences were obtained because of the task, the characteristics of the subjects tested, or that other unknown mediating variables were operative. Subsequent studies investigated the influence of such mediating variables as internal-external control (Martens, 1971) and socioeconomic status (Martens, 1972) as they combined with social reinforcement to affect complex motor skill learning. These studies however also failed to show any effects from the presentation of social reinforcement on the acquisition of a ball-rolling skill.

From these failures it seemed appropriate to conclude that social reinforcements failed to influence the learning of these novel motor skills. However a closer examination of our experimental paradigm was made from an informational point of view. In every experiment knowledge of results was available to each subject after every trial, either intrinsically (could see his performance outcome) or extrinsically (was told by the experimenter). Additionally the subject received kinesthetic feedback. Both knowledge of results and the kinesthetic feedback provided the subject with more specific information about his performance than did the social reinforcers. In other words the social reinforcers informationally were redundant.

Recently, in an attempt to explain similar findings in the social reinforcement literature studying the acquisition of complex verbal responses, Cairns (1963) wrote: "An event acquires and maintains its reinforcement potential only when it provides a reliable and nonredundant signal. Of two stimuli then the one more informative event for the subject should have the strongest reinforcement potential." To further explain the impotency of social reinforcement, Panda states:

If in the past the child has learned that social comments have little information value because of their indiscriminate use and unreliable occurrence he will ignore them and turn to more reliable cues. Thus . . . the frequency of reinforcers is less important, rather more important is how reliable they are used to discriminate the forthcoming positive events and extent to which they are contingent on the child's response. [1971:60.]

In the motor tasks used in these experiments, the information conveyed by praise and reproof was not useful to the subject in modifying his behavior because the visual and kinesthetic feedback and the knowledge of results provided more precise and useful information. Thus in the Martens' experiments social reinforcement was informationally redundant. But is it not possible that the social reinforcement acted as a motivating factor? Stevenson (1965) provided some insight for answering this question when he specified some of the criteria necessary for social reinforcement to influence subjects' responses. Stevenson suggests that a task should not have a clear terminus or product; the completion of a task can in itself be motivating. Furthermore the task should not possess high intrinsic interest. "If interesting tasks are used it is likely that the . . . supportive comments will initially have only a minimal effect and will gain in effectiveness only after the child has played with the materials long enough to become satiated" (pp. 98-99).

Stevenson's task criteria suggest keeping individuals in the dark about the performance criteria and having a not-too-interesting task, otherwise social reinforcements will not be effective because the individuals will be motivated as a result of intrinsic task properties. In the Martens' experiments the subjects were not kept in the dark about their performance, and based upon most subjects' behavior, they were sufficiently motivated to learn the task. Thus when initially learning, subjects were already motivated and did not require or use additional incentives associated with positive and negative social reinforcements.

Alternatively it is possible that subjects were motivated additionally by social reinforcements, but the increased motivation was not reflected in performance changes. When individuals are learning, motivation is only one factor in the process of acquiring the skill; practice, feedback, and other variables also determine performance capability. Thus although subjects may be motivated to perform better through the presentation of social reinforcement during initial acquisition, their maximum response capability as determined by these other factors for that stage of learning is already being approached, and hence, improved performance cannot occur.

Once initial learning has occurred, however, conditions may change. If other forms of feedback remain available, social reinforcement will continue to have no informational value. But also as the task is learned information about the performance becomes less and less important. On the other hand it is likely that once subjects begin to learn the task well and feel they have accomplished their goal, their continued motivation to perform may wane. Perhaps social reinforcement then, even when knowledge of results is available, will serve as an incentive to perform at maximum capability. This notion was examined in a study (Martens, et al., 1972) where knowledge of results was available to each of the college-age males performing a pursuit rotor task. Some limited support was found for the hypothesis that positive social reinforcements have no effect on the early practice trials but after the skill is learned these reinforcements facilitate performance.

Although we can issue our call for additional research, evidence strongly suggests that for the learning of many motor skills, social reinforcement has little direct influence when other forms of feedback are also available. The role of social reinforcers in the absence of other forms of feedback has been shown to be beneficial to performance improvement. However, to facilitate learning the more specific the information as it pertains to the response the more useful it is. It is not uncommon for physical educators and coaches to overlook this point. Far too often we offer some generalized praise or reproof, but do not provide the learner with specific response information. It is difficult to correct an error without having information about its direction and magnitude. Once the task has been learned, social reinforcement may act as an incentive. If the individual is not motivated to perform well at this stage of performance, social reinforcements may be most useful.

Perhaps you may now conclude that social reinforcements should be eliminated when teaching motor skills, but no such interpretation is intended. Social reinforcements may play a very important indirect role in the learning of motor skills. The judicious use of positive social reinforcement is probably very important in the development and maintenance of positive interpersonal relations between the learner and teacher. Although we often overlook this point, in many voluntary learning experiences the development of negative or even neutral interpersonal relations will result in the learner discontinuing his efforts. Possibly good interpersonal relations may indirectly facilitate learning by maintaining a relationship between the teacher and learner in which the learner will heed the information provided him by the teacher.

One of the primary objectives of physical education is to facilitate the acquisition of motor skills through effective instruction. The use of models and social reinforcement are common tools used by physical educators in pursuing these objectives. Why physical education research has not been directed at these obvious and important practical issues is puzzling. Although many questions remain to be answered about social reinforcement as an instructional tool for teaching motor skills, we have at least given some indication of its informational role. To fully understand social reinforcement, the many related variables considered in the verbal and social behavior section in this chapter, and some not reviewed, must also be understood as they pertain to motor behavior. At this time, however, it seems wise to adopt the strategy that the effects will be the same for these various behaviors until shown to be different.

CHAPTER 5

THE PROCESS OF COMPETITION

Competition is a social process that is so pervasive in Western civilization that none can escape it. Indeed the pervasiveness of competition has so polarized our views that some people shun it and others glorify it. Apathy toward competition is not a problem; extreme emotion and irrational thought frequently are.

Competition is generally credited as a potent agent in the socialization of the child and a significant force in motivating behavior. Parents are concerned about competition because they must find answers to such questions as: When do we allow Johnny to begin playing in organized competitive sports? What do we as parents do when he succeeds and when he fails? Should we urge him into competitive programs or do we let him decide? Teachers are concerned about competition, for they must consider answers to such questions as: What are the immediate consequences of competition on the child? Does he learn faster or slower under competitive situations? And what are the long-term effects of competitive programs? That is, how are his motives, attitudes, and personality affected by intensive competitive activities?

The proponents of competition argue that learning to compete is essential to a successful existence in modern society. Usually these proponents suggest that competitive sports programs are excellent training opportunities for learning to experience success and failure, particularly because the consequences are much less severe than in other facets of life. Opponents of competition counter by noting that cooperation is what must be learned to survive in modern society. They point out that all types of competitive programs, including sports programs, have just as important, if not greater, psychological consequences for their participants, than do other facets of life.

Both the proponents and opponents of competition have selected Little League sports programs as the battleground on which to wage their verbal war. The opponents of competition will use examples from Little League to show that intensive competition made Johnny neurotic, that the coach in his zealous desire to win stifled Billy's motivation to succeed, and that both Mom and Dad abused Junior when he played poorly. The advocates of competition retort, however, by observing how competition in Little League developed character in Charlie, made a leader out of Sammy, and changed hostile Harry to a nonviolent, amicable man.

Competition, when discussed in these emotional contexts, is seen in terms of polarities. Competition is either good or bad, or competition is bad and cooperation is good. These simplistic points of view have been largely perpetuated by the writers of popular journals. Almost always these viewpoints are based on limited observations, experiences, or discussions with participants and observers. Almost never are these viewpoints based on any scientific evidence.

To discuss the pros and cons of competition largely from

intuitive or experiential positions has been one approach to the study of competition. We shall not consider it further here for it fails to satisfy the objectives of this text. One of the difficulties with this intuitive approach is that no one bothers to clearly define competition. For us to understand the antecedents and consequences of competition, it is imperative that we have a clear conception of the term *competition*. Therefore considerable space in this chapter will be devoted to understanding what competition is and how it differs from similar phenomena.

The primary focus of this chapter is on *individual* competitive behavior and not on intergroup competition or on cooperation. The basic unit of competition is the individual; in cooperation, the basic unit is the group. Although we will refer to cooperation in this chapter when it helps us understand competition, both cooperation and intergroup competition are discussed more fully in the *Sociology of Sport* text in this series.

DEFINING COMPETITION

Although the term *competition* has some meaning for all of us, it is obvious that it does not mean exactly the same thing to each of us. Competition as a scientific construct is a conceptual disaster primarily because competition research is another area where theory has not played a part. Without the guidance of theory, competition has not been defined rigorously nor has it been operationalized in any standard way. Instead competition has been used to refer to a process, to specific behaviors, to behavioral tendencies, and to specific situations. For competition to become a useful experimental construct it is necessary to distinguish among these uses of competition and to understand their relationship to each other. Henceforth we shall reserve the term *competition* to mean a process. This process is graphically illustrated in Figure 5.1 as a four-category frame of reference with the individual as the focal organism.

Figure 5.1 illustrates the process of competition as involving four stages or categories of events: the objective competitive situation, the subjective competitive situation, the response, and the consequences of the response. These stages are linked to each other as shown by the lines. The links pass through the person, who is the focal organism, illustrating that the individ-

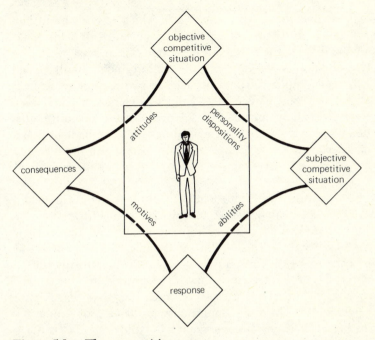

Figure 5.1. The competition process.

ual may and certainly does influence the relationship between each of the stages of the competition process. Some of the personal attributes that may influence various stages of the competition process include attitudes, motives, abilities, previous experiences, and personality dispositions. Of course, each state is influenced by the other stages and also by external factors in the environment. The relationships among these stages are examined more closely below.

Objective Competitive Situation
The first stage of the competitive process is the *objective competitive situation* with which the person is confronted. An objective competitive situation simply refers to those real factors in the physical or social environment that are arbitrarily defined as constituting a competitive situation. The most widely used definition of competition, known as the reward definition,

defines competition as a situation in which rewards to an individual are distributed unequally on the basis of performance among those participating in the activity. In contrast, a cooperative situation is one in which the reinforcements to all individuals depend upon the joint behavior of two or more individuals. (Church, 1968.) When viewed this way competitive and cooperative situations are seen as polarities. In a cooperative situation an individual obtains a reward only if all individuals obtain it, whereas in a competitive situation, if one or a limited number of individuals obtains a reward, the remaining individuals do not.

The reward definition of a competitive situation does not, however, adequately define an objective competitive situation. The reward definition has been found wanting because in many so-called competitive situations it is difficult if not impossible to achieve consensus on the criteria for the distribution of rewards, on the subjective value of the rewards, and on the goal to be achieved. For example, say you are an average tennis player and you have the opportunity to play a professional tennis player. It is obvious you cannot win and your goal is not to do so. You decide that if you can keep from embarrassing yourself by playing reasonably well you will be satisfied. Or perhaps you decide that if you can win two games in a set you will have achieved your goal. It is clear that your goal and the rewards you seek are quite different from your opponent's. Thus defining competition on the basis of rewards has little scientific value for it cannot clearly be operationalized because it requires the experimenter to make assumptions about how each competitor perceives the task and its outcomes. In essence, then, the reward definition of competition does not define an objective competitive situation, but makes inferences about how the subject perceives the objective competitive situation, his response to it, and the consequences of it.

Those using the reward definition as the basis for their study of competition (and almost all researchers have) have operationally defined competitive situations in such diverse ways that some appear to have little similarity to others. Thus it has been nearly impossible to evaluate the literature using the reward definition. Then too the reward definition has not led to any theoretical development, nor does it offer any indication as to why competition occurs.

An alternative definition of an objective competitive situation stems from social evaluation theory (Festinger, 1954; Myers, 1961) and research (Cottrell, 1968; Martens and Landers, 1972). An objective competitive situation is defined as a situation "in which the comparison of an individual's performance is made with some standard in the presence of at least one other person who is aware of the criterion for comparison and can evaluate the comparison process." (Martens, 1971, p. 8.) A standard can be another individual's performance, an idealized performance level, or his own past performance. The primary feature distinguishing a competitive situation from other comparison situations is that the criterion for comparison is known by the person in a position to evaluate the performance.

This definition of an objective competitive situation is an arbitrary one assigned to a particular class of social situations. It includes many social evaluative situations commonly considered to be competitive, but it excludes other evaluative situations. For example, competition does not occur if others present are unaware of the comparison. You may be working toward breaking your own personal record in the high jump while practicing with your teammates, but if they or others observing you are unaware of the comparison, a competitive situation does not exist. Our definition of an objective competitive situation also excludes the comparison of a person's performance with his previous performance in the absence of an evaluative other. For example, you may retreat to your backyard to practice putting, each time taking ten shots from a specified spot. Each time you decide you will improve by one on the number of balls you put into the cup. Is this competition? Some would say yes, but according to our definition it is not.

Sherif (1972) disagrees with these qualifications about the competitive process, although she considers competition to be a social process. Competition in her view "does not require the presence of others, as a person can direct activities toward meeting a standard or achieving a goal that she sets herself, as in practicing a skill . . ." (p. 4). This definition of competition would then incorporate virtually all types of situations, the primary determinant of whether or not a situation is competitive being how the person perceives the situation. As we will discuss shortly, the perception of the situation is very important, but a construct such as competition loses its usefulness when it is so all-inclusive that it excludes nothing. If competition can on the one hand be a social process, but yet totally a private interpretation on the part of each person in response to no particular stimuli, it has no functional value either in describing behavior or in understanding the process. If the competitive process cannot be associated with a particular class of social situations, it becomes only an illusory term to which the identification of antecedents and consequences becomes impossible. Thus it is essential to describe a class of situations that may elicit the competitive process, and these situations must in some way be exclusive of other situations.

Similarly, to philosophically debate the legitimacy of defining an objective competitive situation as being one class of social situations versus another is fruitless. The issue is not the label we attach to this class of social situations. The issue is the understanding of this process as elicited by these particular social situations. The objective competitive situation for that matter could be labeled anything; for example, the objective "evaluative" situation. It is clear, however, that the definition of an objective competitive situation has some basis in reality for it incorporates almost all situations considered by most people to be competitive.

The advantages of defining an objective competitive situation as we have are:

1. The objective competitive situation can be operationalized for careful study.
2. The definition incorporates the great majority of activities commonly thought to be competitive.
3. The definition has theoretical and empirical support from social evaluation theory and research.
4. The definition makes no inferences about the person's perception of the situation, the response made to it, or the consequences of the response.

The process of competition begins by considering the tendencies of the person to seek out objective competitive situations. Many factors within the person will determine his tendency to seek out or avoid competitive situations. We will refer to this tendency as *competitiveness* and it should be viewed as a personality disposition.

Subjective Competitive Situation

A person may find himself in an objective competitive situation either by seeking out the situation or by circumstance. Regardless of how a person is confronted with an objective competitive situation, when he is in this situation he must evaluate the situation in some way. How the person perceives, accepts, and appraises the objective competitive situation is the second stage of the competition process, and is called the *subjective competitive situation*. His evaluation may be largely influenced by whether or not he sought out the objective competitive situation. Thus the person's competitiveness will be an important factor in determining how he appraises an objective competitive situation. But other factors within the person such as motives, attitudes, abilities, and other personality dispositions will also influence the person's appraisal. Additional factors that will determine in part how the person appraises the situation include his perception of the standard to which he expects to make a comparison, his own perceived response capability, and his perception of the importance of the comparison.

Response

When subjectively appraising the competitive situation the person must decide whether he will or will not further participate in the competitive process. That is, he must decide to approach or avoid the objective competitive situation. Assuming he approaches, the third stage of the competition process occurs, which is the person's *response*. The person's response occurs at three levels: physiological, psychological, and behavioral. Responses normally are compared only at the behavioral level, but they may be compared at the other two levels.

A number of internal and external factors may determine the person's response. A person's ability and his motivational level are at least two important internal factors. External factors include such items as the weather, time, facilities, and the opponent's competitive behavior, particularly in an interdependent task; that is, where one person's response is dependent upon the opponent's response.

Consequences

The final category of the competition process is the *consequences* arising from the comparison of the person's response to a standard. We usually dichotomize consequences into being either positive or negative, although supposedly they may be neutral. Again how the person perceives the consequences of the comparison determines its significance for him. For example, to return to our tennis player, although he may have lost the match, if he perceived that he played well, the consequences may have been positive for him rather than negative.

Summary

The process of *competition* occurs each time the person is confronted with an objective competitive situation. *Competitive behavior* includes seeking out objective competitive situations that are determined by the disposition *competitiveness*. Competitive behavior also is the response of the person when he decides to compare his performance to some standard that will be evaluated by another person(s). An additional distinction has been made between competitive behavior and rivalrous behavior. Rivalry, as defined by Mead (1961), is behavior oriented toward another individual in which a favorable comparison is sought, whereas competitive behavior is oriented toward a goal in which others are of secondary importance. Rivalry, then, is people oriented and competitive behavior is task or goal oriented.

Competition as presented in this framework is viewed as a social-psychological construct and is one form of social evaluation. The proper concern of the student of competition is the study of the myriad factors influencing the relationship between the objective competitive situation, the subjective competitive situation, the person's response, and the consequences of the comparison. The complexity of the competition process is surely evident within this model and many factors in understanding this process were not mentioned. The framework attempts to alleviate the conceptual confusion surrounding the term *competition*. Hopefully, with these distinctions, we can better understand some of the determinants and consequences of competitiveness and competitive behavior.

DETERMINANTS OF COMPETITIVE BEHAVIOR

The determinants of any complex social behavior must include consideration of both situational and intrapersonal factors and the relationship between them. The model of the competition process presented earlier should make this evident. Recall that within this model competitive behavior occurs at two points. First, competitive behavior occurs when the person seeks out competitive situations and, second, when the person responds to a competitive situation. This section then will consider some of the determinants of these two forms of competitive behavior.

Although it would be desirable to review many situational as well as intrapersonal factors that influence competitive behavior, the limited research makes this impossible. Because knowledge about why we compete is incomplete, we will focus our attention here on intrapersonal factors only, with particular emphasis on the origins of the disposition we have termed *competitiveness*.

Before proceeding it is important to recognize that the process of competition cannot begin until children have reached certain levels of cognitive maturity. Sherif (1971) notes that the competition process requires an individual to have the capacity to direct behavior consistently toward an abstract standard or remote goal. This capacity appears to emerge between the ages of 3 to 5 years. (Greenberg, 1952; Heckhausen, 1967.) Although the competition process cannot occur until a certain level of cognitive maturity is reached, this does not imply that through the socialization process, competitiveness is not being shaped in the child under 3.

Now we can return to the question: What motivates man to compete? One answer has been that competitive behavior is instinctual. Earlier in this century it was widely accepted that man has an innate drive to strive for objects that cannot be possessed in common. In fact this view is not rejected today. Singer (1968) in discussing the differences between competition and cooperation wrote: "Competition is more of a basic or primitive instinct; cooperation involves greater degrees of maturation and intellectual involvement" (p. 255). To attribute human competitiveness solely to instinctual mechanisms does not answer such questions as: What makes one man so much more competitive than another? What makes one ethnic, religious, or racial group more competitive than another? Why are Mexicans less competitive than Anglo-Americans? Although competitiveness may have a genetic base, it is largely determined by previous experiences, cultural influences, parental and peer influences, or in general by the social environment. Competitiveness in fact is simply a personality disposition and can be influenced by the myriad experiences that help shape any personality disposition.

We use the term *competitiveness* to encompass a cluster of motives that predispose an individual to compete or not to compete. Experimental research with the construct need achievement or achievement motivation indicates that competitiveness is closely related to, if not a part of, achievement motivation. Achievement motivation is a system of goal-direction in human activity that is closely related to competence, aggressiveness, and dominance. High levels of achievement motivation may stem from a composite of anxiety and fear of failure, a desire for mastery and competence of the environment, a desire for power over others, or competitive desires to excel the performance of others.

Although competitiveness and achievement motivation are closely related, an important distinction exists. Achievement motivation is a broad system of goal-direction and does not imply any particular mode in which achievement may be directed. Competitiveness, however, implies a motive to achieve or succeed, and also implies that this achievement will be sought through objective competitive situations. Thus the prime distinction between competitiveness and achievement motivation is that competitiveness is a disposition to select objective competitive situations as the mode for achieving. Some evidence to support such a distinction has been obtained by Maehr and Sjogren (1971) and Veroff (1969).

Development of Competitiveness

Although a conceptual distinction has been made between achievement motivation and competitiveness, their origin most likely is similar. Therefore we will briefly consider achievement motivation's origins and then consider what predisposes a person to select competitive situations in seeking achievement. As we observed earlier for competitiveness, Heckhausen comments that the origin of achievement motivation

> . . . lies neither in the appearance of something laid down innately nor in the descent from ontogenetically earlier motives, as has been vaguely assumed. . . . Rather it appears along with the cognitive step in maturing. . . . As a rule, this step is not taken before the age of three as has been confirmed by other research on competition among small children of that age. . . ." [1967:143.]

Veroff (1969) has described three stages that the child experiences in the development of achievement motivation. First, the child strives for what is called "autonomous competence." In this stage the child is striving to master his environment. His achievement goals are intrinsic and he makes comparisons with his own norms, not those set by others. The emergence of autonomous competence in the child is dependent upon the development of a primitive evaluative system for making these comparisons.

The second stage of development is concerned with social comparison or social achievement motivation. Veroff views this stage as an opportunity for the child to learn about himself in relation to the world. Now the child compares himself with the norms set by others, not his own norms. Veroff believes that autonomous competence begins as early as 2 years and that social comparison does not begin until about 5 or 6 years.

The third stage occurs when autonomous achievement motivation is integrated with social comparison strivings. According to Veroff, successful mastery of each stage must occur before the child can master the next stage. For mastery of the first stage to occur the child needs freedom of access to the environment, sufficient exposure to stimulation requiring autonomous mastery, and sufficient parental support for autonomous action. Successful mastery of social comparison requires a child "to compare favorably with a reasonably large majority of others of the same age and sex with respect to the valued attributes of the social group to which he refers himself." (Veroff, 1969, p. 54.) For successful mastery of the integration of autonomous and social comparison motivation a child needs to establish a strong sense of independence. In appropriate situations he needs to recognize his own effectiveness apart from the social groups to which he belongs.

Within Veroff's developmental scheme, competition emerges in the social comparison stage and is integrated into other comparison forms, primarily nonsocial comparisons in the third stage. Veroff postulates that the successful integration of these comparison forms occurs most frequently in the middle teen years.

Additional evidence on the development of the achievement motive verifies the importance of the sociocultural milieu, including social class, educational level, and religion. Upwardly mobile middle class favors the development of high achievement motivation. Achievement motivation is positively correlated with the parents' education level. The Catholic milieu is less favorable for the development of high achievement motivation than is the Protestant (Heckhausen, 1967). Further evidence indicates that parental influence is important in shaping the achievement motive. Mothers who strive for early independence training rear children with higher levels of achievement motivation than do mothers who restrict their child's behavior. Additionally, firstborn children in a family, males more than females, higher socioeconomic groups, and the members of ethnic and racial majorities in our society are more achievement motivated than their counterparts. Further evidence summarized by Smith (1969) led him to conclude that high achievement motivation is associated with "(1) relatively early demands for accomplishment, (2) affectively intense rewards for accomplishment such as physical affection or praise, (3) relatively high goals set for children by parents, (4) a favorable parental view of . . . competence, and (5) interest and involvement in [a child's] achievement endeavors" (p. 109).

As we have already learned from Veroff then, the origins of

competitiveness are rooted in the development of achievement motivation; competitiveness being one stage of development toward an integrated autonomous achievement person. Similarly Maehr and Sjogren (1971) suggest that there simply may be two types of achievement motivation persons which they call self-competitive and socially competitive. Similar to Veroff's autonomous competence stage, early the child strives for competence or self-competitive comparisons (not competitive behavior as defined in this chapter, but instead is known as self-evaluation) and is not interested in social comparisons. But later Maehr and Sjogren (1971) state ". . . during middle childhood when social comparison processes become both possible and important, achievement motivation may be exhibited in an inclination toward socially competitive patterns" (p. 149).

The little experimental evidence available on the development of the competitiveness disposition comes from the work of Madsen and his colleagues (Nelson and Kagan, 1972). They have focused primarily on cross-cultural studies to determine how children in our society differ from other societies in competitiveness. Their work has shown that Anglo-American children are more competitive than Mexican children, but that urban children in Canada, Holland, Israel, and Korea are all similarly competitive to Anglo-American children. Rural children in all cultures were less competitive than urban children. Additionally Nelson and Kagan (1972) observed that Anglo-American children are more rivalrous than rural Mexican children. They commented on this fact by saying, "Anglo-American children are not only irrationally competitive, they are almost sadistically rivalrous." One explanation offered for these differences is that rural Mexican mothers tend to reinforce their children noncontingently, that is, rewarding them whether or not they succeed, whereas Anglo-American mothers tend to reinforce their children as a rigid function of the child's achievement.

CONSEQUENCES OF COMPETITION

As mentioned earlier, the consequences accruing from engaging in the competition process can be classified as either positive or negative. Furthermore these positive and negative outcomes may be in terms of performance effects, intrapersonal effects, and interpersonal effects. Much more research has been directed toward understanding the performance effects, but there is considerable speculation about the intra- and interpersonal effects.

Intrapersonal Effects

Some of the important questions related to intrapersonal factors include: What is the influence of success and failure experiences on such intrapersonal dimensions as attitudes, motives, and personality dispositions? Specifically, of considerable interest is how previous competitive experiences influence the development of the personality disposition competitiveness. Another important question is how the evaluative dimension of competition influences the person's conception of himself. What attitudes does the person develop about the competitive task and about those with whom he interacts? How satisfied is he or she with a competitive experience? Some discussion of the influence of competition on intrapersonal factors is undertaken in the socialization section later, particularly when discussing aggression, attitudes, and personality. But, in general, the answers to these questions remain unknown at this time.

Interpersonal Effects

Considerable interest has been shown in learning about the influence of competition on interpersonal factors, although far too little is known. Interpersonal factors refer to those variables that influence the relationship and interpersonal exchange between two or more individuals. From a physical education standpoint we are primarily interested in how participation in competition facilitates the development of interpersonal competence. For example, research has shown that through competition, members of the same team develop a strong attraction for each other, which in part leads to a more cohesive team. Success in competition of course augments this attraction and the resultant cohesion, more so than failure. Current research is just beginning to identify what in the competition process leads to heightened interpersonal attraction.

Evidence also reveals that after competing, competitors have a stronger attraction for opponents if they are of similar ability. On the other hand, some evidence indicates that we are attracted to people who are competent. Thus we may have a stronger attraction for those who are somewhat better than us than to those who are less able than us.

We began this chapter by noting that much has been said about how interpersonal skills can be developed through the competition process. And of course this cannot be denied, but neither can it be substantiated by empirical evidence. Potentially we can learn much about how to effectively interact with people by engaging in the competitive process, just as we can by engaging in any social process. The question then is not whether competition improves our interpersonal competence, but how we can maximize the acquisition of interpersonal competence through the competitive process. An understanding of the mechanisms of observational learning, social reinforcement, and the entire socialization process will help in part to answer these questions. But specific work in the competitive situation is also needed.

Performance Effects

Because of the direction of previous research, we have considerably more information about the effects of competition on motor performance. Nearly 25 studies have examined the effects of a competitive situation on motor performance. Although the generalizations are rather tenuous, evidence suggests that competitive situations facilitate performance on muscular endurance and strength tasks, as well as on well-learned and simple skills. Competitive situations appear to impair performance, however, on complex tasks or tasks not well learned. These generalizations are identical to those found in the social facilitation area, suggesting that competitive situations have some similarity to audience and coaction effects. And of course they do. As was learned earlier, the critical element in social facilitation is evaluation potential. The operational definition of almost all competition investigations has also included the potential for evaluation (and of course the definition of an objective competitive situation used in this chapter includes evaluation). Until evidence suggests otherwise, it is parsimonious to consider the effects of competition on motor performance to be similar to social facilitation effects.

Two personality factors, trait anxiety and achievement motivation, have been studied as mediators of competitive effects on motor performance. Trait anxiety is a predisposition to respond with heightened arousal to certain classes of stimuli. Three studies have investigated the effects of competitive situations on high and low trait anxiety subjects. One study found that low anxious subjects performed better than high anxious subjects in a competitive situation (Vaught and Newman, 1966), another study found the opposite (McGowan, 1968), and a third found no differences (Martens and Landers, 1969). These equivocal findings parallel the studies examining the relationship between anxiety and audience presence.

Ryan and Lakie (1965) investigated performance on a ringpeg task in competitive and noncompetitive situations among college males who varied both in achievement motivation and trait anxiety. They found that high anxiety-low achievement motivation subjects performed significantly better in the noncompetitive situations than the low anxiety-high achievement motivation subjects. The opposite, however, was true in the competitive situation.

Competitive situations, as most of us know, can at times produce considerable stress in a person. Competitive stress can be defined as a perceived imbalance between the demand or expectation of the objective competitive situation and the response capability of the person, under conditions where failure to meet the demand has important consequences for the person.[2] Although competitive stress is pervasive, particularly in sports, it has been difficult to study this phenomenon experimentally. The primary problem is creating competitive stress in the laboratory to a sufficient intensity level to approximate a real-life situation. Other problems include determining exactly which competitive situations are stressful for which subjects and in quantifying the degree of stress.

---

[2] This definition is modified from McGrath's (1970, p. 20) general definition of stress.

It has been well established that stress manifests heightened arousal. Hence to explain the relationship between performance and arousal as manifested by competitive stress, we return to the inverted-U hypothesis (see Figure 2.1). This hypothesis, it will be recalled, simply suggests that the quality of performance increases with stress up to some optimal point, whereupon additional increase in stress will decrease performance quality.

One of the few and probably the best tests of the inverted-U hypothesis for competitive stress was completed by Lowe (1973) on Little League baseball teams. Competitive stress was quantified by the criticalness of the game in relationship to the other games of the season (game criticality), and the criticalness of the situation within any one game (situation criticality). Game criticality increased, for example, when the two teams playing each other were closer in the league standings and nearer first place, and the number of remaining games was small. Situation criticality increased as the innings became fewer, the score closer, the number of outs greater, and the number and position of players on base higher. Lowe, however, did not simply assume that these situations would be more stressful. He obtained both physiological and observational data to corroborate his belief that competitive stress increased arousal as the criticalness of the game and situation increased.

Lowe analyzed the hitting performance of the Little Leaguers as a function of the variation in game and situation criticality. The results supported the inverted-U hypothesis. Little Leaguers performed best under moderate levels of stress as compared to very high and low levels of stress. Besides the findings of this study, the methodology is worth noting. Lowe's study of Little League sport competition is an excellent example of how stress can be quantified by systematic changes in the competitive situation. Further research of this form will be most useful in understanding the complex process of competition and in overcoming the problems of laboratory research

Several other research findings warrant attention. Wankel (1969) examined the interaction between ability level and competition when performing a balancing task. The results supported Zajonc's hypothesis. The noncompetitive groups per-

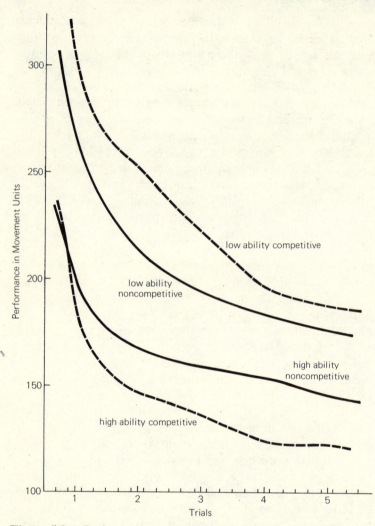

Figure 5.2. Performance curves from the Wankel (1969) study.

formed best early and the competitive groups performed best after considerable practice. The high ability-competitive group performed best for all the practice trials and the low ability-competitive group performed poorest. Thus initial ability plays an important role in determining the effects of competition on performance.

A related finding is that competitive situations increase the speed of a response but not the quality of the response. (Whittemore, 1924; Church, 1968.) Although the speed of a response appears to be increased in the competitive situation, the magnitude of the facilitation is likely to be related to the probability of success. Church (1968) tested this notion, finding that response rate on a lever pressing task improved when the probability of success was 50 percent or less over those with the probability of success of 80 percent.

The same hypothesis was elaborated upon by Swingle (1969). The subjects raced against a computer-programmed opponent by moving a lever manually. The study determined the subject's speed of response when he won 10 percent, 50 percent, or 90 percent of the time under low- and high-challenge conditions. In the low challenge conditions the subject always lagged considerably behind the computer-controlled opponent. In the high challenge condition he was always behind but only by a very small distance. The results showed that the subject who won 50 percent responded faster under high challenge than under low challenge, that subjects who won 10 percent responded faster under low challenge than high challenge, and that challenge had no effect on the 90 percent win group.

We have reviewed some of the more noteworthy findings with respect to the effects of competition on motor performance It is risky business, however, because of the diverse ways in which competition has been operationally defined. Although still unknown, the variation in experimental findings must be due in part to these differences. For example, some studies have not actually created different social situations; they attempted to manipulate competition by reading instructions to the subject that directed him to compete. Other studies that have varied the objective competitive situation have given little concern as to how the subject appraised the competitive situation. Although a particular social situation is presented to the person, and the experimenter labels it competitive, the subject may not so perceive it. The primary reason for these difficulties is the conceptual confusion plaguing the concept of competition.

Successfully understanding competition requires first a clear definition of the constructs that are integral to the competition process. Second, it is necessary to develop a framework that hypothesizes how these constructs are related to each other. Third, it is vital to test these hypothesized relationships to discern their validity. This chapter has attempted to do the first and in part the second; the third remains to be done. While some evidence is available, much of the competition research is inadequate. Both the determinants and the consequences of competition need wide-scale study.

PART III

SOCIALIZATION AND PHYSICAL ACTIVITY

Each of us must learn many things to become useful members of society. The process by which we learn to become competent members of society is known as *socialization*. Because socialization is a manifestly broad and general concept, interest in socialization has not been limited to the field of social psychology, but has been of intimate concern to cultural anthropology and sociology as well as to applied fields, including education and physical education. Socialization indeed has been a common focal point for all behavioral sciences.

Physical educators and recreators frequently have claimed that physical activities, particularly sports, are among the more effective means for socializing the young members of our society. By this they mean that participation in physical activities helps to develop interpersonal competencies. But in Chapter 6 we shall see that socialization has a much broader meaning than just the development of interpersonal competence. In this chapter a brief overview of the socialization process is presented followed by a discussion of the influence of the socialization process on the acquisition of skills and knowledge about physical fitness and movement. In Chapter 7 we will be concerned with the influence of physical activity on the development of interpersonal competence.

In their concern for the development of a socially competent person, physical educators have been particularly interested in three social variables: aggression, attitudes, and personality. Among the most important socialization problems facing man today is learning to control aggression. In Chapter 8 we examine the role of physical activity, particularly sport, as a socialization agency for the control of aggression. Another important function of the socialization process is the development of socially desirable attitudes and personality dispositions. In Chapters 9 and 10, respectively, we review each of these topics as they relate to physical activity.

CHAPTER 6 | THE SOCIALIZATION PROCESS

As a child grows he learns many things. He learns how to walk and talk, he learns how to write and do arithmetic, how to obtain rewards and avoid punishments. He learns how to play with others, how to sing, and tell stories. He learns how to ride a bicycle, play baseball, and eventually drive a car. He learns to be friendly or hostile, modest or bold, sympathetic or dispassionate.

In general the growing child learns the patterns of behavior that are common in his society, or what we call *norms*. He also learns that society has certain *values* or ideas that are held to be right or wrong. He discovers that society has a social structure in which

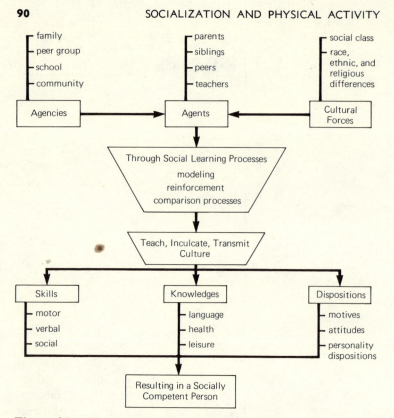

Figure 6.1. The socialization process.

people have different statuses and roles. *Status* is a position in the social structure and a *role* is the expected behavior of a person occupying a particular status. The child soon becomes aware that he too has certain statuses in the social structure and that with every status he has certain rights and obligations. For example, in the child-parent relationship he has the right to be protected and provided for by his mother and father, but has the obligation to obey their instructions.

Socialization then is the process by which the child learns these things. It is "the process by which a society trains its children to behave like adults" (Baldwin, 1968, p. 439). In Figure 6.1 the socialization process is depicted showing the various components which, if the process is successful, result in a socially competent person. Figure 6.1 is not meant to be inclusive but exemplary of the primary components of the socialization process. Society's objective through the socialization process is to produce a competent person. *Competence* in this sense means the ability to effectively interact with one's environment, both physical and social. To function effectively in any society the person must acquire a broad range of skills, knowledge, and dispositions. The key to the acquisition of these skills, knowledge, and dispositions is *social learning*, a process that is contrasted with maturation. Maturation is the unfolding of the potentialities of the organism that occurs more or less automatically. Social learning, in contrast, is learning a society's culture through the processes of reinforcement, particularly social reinforcement; modeling or observational learning; and social comparison processes, including competition. A society's *culture* is the sum total of socially transmitted behavior patterns, arts, beliefs, institutions, and all other products of society that are passed on from generation to generation. Culture provides man with a coherent outlook and approach to life; it provides social reality. Through such agencies as the family, peer group, the school, and the community, and under the influence of cultural forces such as social class, race, ethnic, and religious differences, the socialization agents of a society teach, inculcate, and transmit our culture. These socialization agents may be any member of society, but for the young the primary agents are parents, siblings, peers, and teachers.

The effectiveness of the socialization process may be evaluated in terms of the person's ability to successfully function in many social roles; that is, to be socially competent. Competence then involves effective role performance in terms of how society defines competence. Competence, in the form of certain skills, may be valued in one society and not in another. For example, the ability to throw a spear accurately may be a skill required of adult males in a primitive African society, but has no value in making an adult American male competent in our society. Instead the skill of driving an automobile is almost essential in our society, but would have little relevance for a primitive African.

A frequent misconception about socialization is that this

process is concerned only with developing interpersonal skills or competencies. This is a myopic view of what the socialization process transmits and inculcates to a societal member. The socialization process is not only concerned with developing interpersonal skills but many other skills, knowledge, and dispositions, all of which help to make the person a socially competent member of his society. Thus an important distinction is made between what we will term *interpersonal competence* and *social competence*. Interpersonal competence refers to interpersonal skills, certain attitudes and personality dispositions that facilitate interpersonal relations. Other skills and knowledge, however, such as motor skills and language skills also must be acquired for a person to be socially competent; that is, to function effectively in society.

The learning of society's culture (skills, knowledge, and dispositions) through the socialization process obviously is interdependent on the development of each component. For example, the young child who is slow to develop certain motor skills finds it difficult to enter peer groups because he is not competent in running, climbing, and in other motor skills valued by his peer group. He finds himself isolated from his peers, and thus has less opportunity to develop social skills arising through peer-group interaction. Conversely, the child may be quite competent in running, throwing, and hitting a ball, but his incompetencies in social skills cause him to be rejected by the peer group.

Another misconception about the socialization process is that it is restricted to childhood and adolescence. Socialization, however, is a continuous process throughout life because the demands of society change with time, just as the person changes with time. Physical changes in the adult (e.g., changes in health and energy level) necessitate continued socialization or the learning of new social roles. Socialization is also important for the adult in acquiring an occupation, and with rapid technological changes the adult may need to learn a new occupation several times in his life. In making occupational changes adults may have to learn new interpersonal skills as well as new work skills. The adult also experiences many changes when leaving his maternal family and establishing his own family. Socialization is an important part of a marriage and of parenthood. Children, divorce, and death within the family place different social demands on a person, and thus require learning new social roles. Although little attention has been directed to studying adult socialization with the average person, considerable attention has been directed toward the deviant adult: the criminal, the drug addict, the alcoholic, and the emotionally ill. The role of physical education and physical activities in the socialization of adults has been ignored completely. Similar to the general socialization research, physical educators' limited interest in the socialization process has been with the problem of pre-adult socialization.

THE SOCIALIZATION PROCESS AND THE
ACQUISITION OF SKILLS AND KNOWLEDGE
ABOUT PHYSICAL FITNESS AND MOVEMENT

We have described socialization as the process by which society transmits its culture to its members so that they may learn to function as competent members of the society. As an agency of society and as part of the educational system, the *primary* socialization function of physical education is the teaching of skills and knowledge about physical fitness and movement. A *secondary* or collateral socialization function of physical education is the development of interpersonal competence. The secondary socialization function receives considerable attention in the remaining chapters of this book. In this section we give limited attention to how the socialization process functions in transmitting skills and knowledge about physical fitness and movement to the members of our society.

The teaching of skills and knowledge about physical fitness and movement is done by agents of society through various learning processes, particularly social learning processes that consist largely of modeling, reinforcement, and comparison processes. Part II focused on these social learning processes as they influence motor behavior. Therefore in this section we will focus our attention on a limited number of cultural forces, agencies, and agents of society. The student interested in studying these elements of society will find a very fertile field; research is almost nonexistent, and most of the research available is of questionable value. Consequently, we are able to introduce only briefly some of the more obvious cultural forces, agencies, and agents, and raise some questions about their relationship to physical activity.

Before proceeding we should recognize that sport sociologists have shown considerable interest in the socialization process. Their primary concern has been with the influence that various components of the socialization process have on the preference for sport involvement and with how social roles are learned in specific sports. These issues will not be considered here for they receive attention in the *Sociology of Sport* text in this series.

Cultural Forces

Among the important cultural forces operative in any society are social class and ethnic or minority group differences. Although the concept of social class is repugnant to some, most people recognize that different groups possess unequal amounts of wealth, influence, prestige, and opportunity. Social class is usually divided into upper, middle, and lower class and is commonly determined by various indices, which include one or more of the following factors: educational level, father's occupation, family income, and location of residence. The importance of social class is in understanding how differences among classes differentially influence the socialization of members within each class. Important differences have been shown in:

1. The types of learning experiences to which a person is exposed. For example, the quality of family relationships and the patterns of affection and authority in the family vary substantially among the classes.
2. The conception of the self.
3. The way attitudes and personality dispositions are developed.
4. The goals that a person sets.

Studies investigating the relationship between social class and measures of motor skill and physical fitness have not been conclusive. Ponthieux and Barker (1965), for example, reported that lower class girls were faster, better coordinated, and had more endurance. On the other hand, upper class girls were found to be stronger in arm and shoulder girdle strength, in abdominal and hip flexor muscles, and in muscular explosiveness. Lower class boys were faster and better coordinated, but upper class boys were superior in combined agility and speed and in strength of abdominal and hip flexor muscles. These findings were statistically marginal, however, and were not substantiated by Young (1969), Young (1970), and Thomas (1969).

Although we do not have enough evidence to reach any conclusions about the relationship between social class and measures of motor skill and physical fitness, it is unlikely that investigations that pursue the mere identification of differences in physical fitness and motor competency will be helpful. First, social class may only be important when interacting with other variables. For example, Rosenhan (1966) has found that social approval facilitated the performance of lower class boys and disapproval impaired their performance more than it did for middle class boys. Possibly then the use of different forms of social reinforcement among various social classes will have different effects on the acquisition of motor skills. Secondly, what is important is *how* social class differences influence motor behavior and physical fitness. Do families of different social classes encourage their members to be more or less physically active? Are different types of motor skills valued more or less by certain social classes? Do peer groups in different social classes encourage the acquisition of certain motor skills? Do families from different classes provide more or less opportunity to participate in certain physical activities? Answering questions similar to these will provide some insight into why (or if) social class differences influence motor competency or physical fitness. In other words, the relationship between social class and motor behavior or physical fitness will be better understood if studied in reference to the total socialization process.

Ethnic differences are also important in the socialization process because members of ethnic groups learn skills, knowledge, and dispositions unique to that subcultural group. Frequently these cultural differences conflict with the norms and values of the larger society. When they do the ethnic group is subjected to unequal treatment, usually receiving inferior status and roles in the social structure of society. Collaterally, minority groups frequently are denied equal access to the material goods of the society as well as to many cultural experiences and opportunities. Besides restricting minority groups' opportunity to learn the norms and values of the larger society, these material and social deprivations may affect a person's psychological makeup, particularly his self-concept, personality, and attitudes. Thus not only are the members of a minority or ethnic group socialized in a culturally distinct group, but they are discriminated against for these differences by other socialization agents of society who should be instrumental in socializing these people into the larger society.

Are ethnic differences, and the corresponding differences in socialization patterns, related to differences in minority members' motor competency or physical fitness? As might be expected the limited research on this question has been mostly with blacks. For various measures of physical fitness, several studies have found blacks to be slightly superior to whites. Barker and Ponthieux (1968) hypothesized that these differences may be attributed to differences in social class. Blacks, however, remained superior to whites on these fitness measures when social class was equated. The major interpretive problems with these findings is knowing whether the differences should be attributed to genetic or environmental factors, or both.

When blacks have been compared with whites on certain motor skills, usually negligible differences have been revealed. One interesting difference found, however, is that whites tend to excel at self-paced activities and blacks tend to excel at reactive activities. (Worthy and Markle, 1970.) Golf and bowling are examples of self-paced sports; these are activities in which the player responds at his own pace. Wrestling and a handball volley are examples of reactive activities; the player must respond to changing stimuli. Unfortunately, satisfactory explanations to account for these differences are unavailable as yet.

Agents and Agencies

Just as the evidence related to the influence of cultural forces is meager, our understanding of the influence of such agencies as the family, peer group, and school, and of such agents as parents, siblings, peers, and teachers on motor skill learning is largely intuitive or based on experience. The varying patterns of parent-child relationships, the interactions of peers, and the teacher-student interaction all appear to be direct or indirect determinants in the acquisition of skills and knowledge of fitness and movement. Understanding the complex interaction among social-environmental factors that may influence the child's motor and physical development is obviously important if physical educators wish to design curricula that help to develop socially competent people. Below we will briefly consider three sets of agencies and agents:

1. The family as an agency and parents as socialization agents.
2. The peer group as an agency and peers as socialization agents.
3. The school as an agency and teachers as socialization agents.

Obviously the family is the first and most important socialization agency. Parents' attempts to socialize their children are determined by what they think the child ought to be, and these attempts in turn are influenced by the social settings within which the family lives. Some of the behavior patterns that a child learns in the family are characteristic of the larger culture and others are unique to the particular family. Through interaction with family members, the child learns values, sentiments, and status expectations. The mechanisms of socialization—reinforcement, modeling, and comparison processes—are first introduced to the child in the family. The child receives his first rewards and punishments, views his first models of behavior, and makes his first comparisons all within the family. Because of the heavy burden of responsibility on the family for socializing the young, it would be expected that social learning would be a planned deliberate effort, but instead social learning is more incidental than planned.

The family influences everything the child does because he initially is totally dependent upon his parents. Obviously then the family influences the child's early development of motor competencies and interest in physical activities. The important question becomes then, *how* does the family influence the development of motor competencies and physical fitness? Whether these influences are direct through reinforcement or modeling procedures, or whether they are indirect through the development of certain attitudes and personality dispositions is not clear. Perhaps the interest in physical activities is associated with the availability of space and equipment provided by parents. More than likely it is a combination of these factors.

In general, because children tend to be like their parents, we can expect that parents who reward the acquisition of motor skills, who value physical fitness, and who themselves engage in physical activities will have children who are more competent and interested in physical activity. This generalization, however, contains too many exceptions to be satisfactory. Many specific questions need answers. For example, what types of parent-child relationships foster the development of wholesome concepts about the self, the body, and engagement in physical activity? Which parent is most influential in the development of these concepts for the different sexes? What is the influence of siblings, sibling's sex, and birth order on the acquisition of motor skills and interest in physical activities? These questions warrant our efforts to answer them.

The peer group is quite different from that of the family, and has certain distinctive functions in socializing the child. These functions include:

1. Giving the child experience in egalitarian types of relationships;
2. Teaching "taboo" subjects;
3. Expanding the social horizons of the child;
4. Encouraging the development of independence;
5. Helping to establish the child's identity or self-concept;
6. Providing opportunity for group expression.

The peer group has its own norms and values. Acceptance in and rejection from peer groups are largely determined by the ability to learn these norms and in the acceptance of the peer groups' values. These norms and values have strong influences on the person's behavior, attitudes, and personality. Through the same social learning mechanisms the peer group can be an important reinforcer and model for the acquisition of motor skills and in shaping attitudes about physical activity in general. Again, however, many specific questions remain unanswered, primarily because research has not been concerned with these issues.

The final agency we will consider is the school, which is recognized as a formal institution of society for socializing its members. The school's primary function is to transmit basic skills and knowledge to its students. In addition to the "three Rs," many less obvious skills, knowledge, and dispositions are intended to be transmitted by the school. In fact the school has an increasing responsibility throughout this century for socializing the young members of society. The teacher, as the agent of the school, obviously serves as an important model and reinforcer for the development of a wide range of skills, knowledge, and dispositions.

As mentioned previously, physical education is a unit of the school whose primary socialization function is the transmission of skills and knowledge about physical fitness and movement. Other agencies of society of course are also important in teaching these skills and knowledge, but their acquisition is a collateral or secondary function of these agencies. An important question then is, "How successful is physical education in accomplishing its primary socialization function?" Do other agencies such as the family, peer groups, and other sport or recreational organizations contribute more or less than physical education to accomplishing this function?

It is difficult to dispute that physical education programs have been somewhat successful in achieving their primary socialization function, but we have not attempted to compare physical education's contribution with other agencies of society. Thus it becomes impossible at this time to evaluate physical education's contribution to society in terms of its success in accomplishing its primary socialization function. Consequently, physical educators often suggest that they too develop good traits such as self-esteem, self-confidence, tolerance, positive personality dispositions, cooperation, and benevolent attitudes (or what we have termed interpersonal competence). When physical educators discuss socialization they often appear to overlook or de-emphasize their primary socialization function and overemphasize collateral or secondary functions. We now turn our attention to these secondary socialization functions.

CHAPTER 7 | INTERPERSONAL COMPETENCE

Interpersonal competence refers to the ability to effectively interact with others. In this chapter we will be concerned with the influence of physical activity on the development of the skills necessary for effective interpersonal relations.

Probably few persons would deny that physical activities, including organized sports, have the *potential* for developing interpersonal competence. Participation in physical activities—including games, play, and sport—provides the opportunity for considerable social interaction under a wide range of situations. Certainly positive social learning may occur from such participation, but negative social behavior may also be acquired. Unfortunately, most of the literature in this area has been mission-oriented; that is, writers have sought to prove that participation in these activities inevitably leads to positive social learning, while ignoring the possibility that it may lead to negative social learning.

For example Helanko (1957) has suggested that sports have been developed by society for the specific purpose of developing interpersonal competence in young people. He writes, "If sports could suddenly be blotted out from the world and from people's consciousness, they would soon be born again and would perhaps even be recreated in the same forms as now, provided that the process of socialization and its influencing factors remained the same." Others also have taken the position that all societies use physical activities—including games, play, and sports—as important means for socializing the young.

GAMES AS SOCIALIZATION MODELS

Moore and Anderson (1969) have hypothesized that in every society man has developed relatively abstract models that have been invented for the expressed purpose of socializing the young. These models serve the function of familiarizing new members of society with the most important features of man's relation to his environment. Accordingly Moore and Anderson see:

1. *Puzzles* as models for the relationship between man and nature; that is, those relations between man and his environment that are not due to chance or luck.
2. *Games of chance* as models for the relationship between man and uncertain aspects of his existence.
3. *Games of strategy* as models for the relationship between man and his interactions with other men.
4. *Aesthetic entities*, or art forms, which give man the opportunity to make normative judgments or evaluations of his experiences.

Moore and Anderson (1969) suggest that "all societies make use of these folk models in the socialization of the young and for the recreation, or recreational enjoyment, of those who are older. Simple forms of these models are internalized in childhood and more complex versions of them sustain us in adulthood" (p. 573).

The importance of physical activities, particularly games, as methods of acquiring interpersonal competence has received additional attention in several cross-cultural studies. Roberts et al. (1959) have found evidence that suggests that various kinds of games serve as opportunities to master various parts of the environment. They proposed that games of strategy were related to mastery of the social system, games of physical skill were associated with mastery of the physical environment, and games of chance were related to familiarity with the supernatural. Roberts and Sutton-Smith (1962) used these game categories in their analysis of the child-rearing practices of 111 societies. Their findings in part confirm Roberts et al.'s (1959) earlier proposal and in part supplements or replaces it with evidence of additional motivational themes. Basically, they found that:

1. Societies stressing obedience training emphasized games of strategy.
2. Societies emphasizing responsibility training stressed games of chance.
3. Societies more concerned with achievement training emphasized games of physical skill.

These findings were then used to predict game preferences among segments of our society that could be differentiated on these three child-rearing dimensions. Sutton-Smith et al. (1963) confirmed the prediction within our society for boys versus girls, and among adults who differed by sex, education, and occupation. Thus the combined within- and cross-cultural findings certainly indicate a positive relationship between these games and the development of interpersonal competence. Unfortunately, however, they provide no insight into *how* these activities are utilized for the acquisition of interpersonal competencies, nor do they provide any indication whatsoever of exactly how successful these societies are in their development of interpersonal competence among individuals.

SOME EVIDENCE—SOME GENERALIZATIONS

Reference to interpersonal competence in the physical education literature has been frequent, but social development, emotional development, and social adjustment have been the terms used. Many of the investigations dealing with the contributions of physical activity to the development of interpersonal competence have been reviewed by Cowell (1960) and Layman (1960, 1970). Although Cowell sought evidence to show that physical activity contributed to the development of interpersonal competence, he was only able at best to establish that a moderate relationship exists between several social variables and participation in physical activity.

Layman (1970), relying on similar evidence as reviewed by Cowell, attempted to substantiate the following propositions:

1. Engaging in sports promotes physical fitness; physical fitness is associated with good emotional health and a lack of fitness with poor emotional health.
2. The acquisition of the motor skills involved in sports contributes toward meeting the basic needs of safety and esteem in young children of both sexes and in boys and young men from the early grades through college years.
3. Supervised play presents potentialities for promoting emotional health and preventing delinquency.
4. . . . when play, recreation, and athletic activities are planned with individual needs in mind, they may be very valuable means of improving emotional health among emotionally ill patients.
5. Play and sport supply outlets for the expression of emotion, and outward expression of emotion in approved activities is conducive to the development and maintenance of emotional health.
6. Competitive sports, if properly used, may enhance emotional health and the acquisition of desirable personality traits.

Unfortunately the research evidence presented by Cowell (1960) and Layman (1960, 1970) does not substantiate these generalizations. The evidence is very weak and is largely correlational; that is, it only suggests that a relationship exists between some interpersonal skills and physical activity, but it does not show that participation in physical activities *causes* the development of interpersonal competence. Physical educators' overconcern with justifying that they *do* develop interpersonal competence has diverted them from investigating *how* they may develop interpersonal competence. Broad generalizations about the development of interpersonal competence through physical activities serve only public relations purposes and not the purpose of improving curricula. And all too often these generalizations are seen through and challenged by those whose support physical education needs. This is not to say that Layman's statements are untrue, for they have some intuitive plausibility, but we must be cautious in distinguishing between what we know and what we think is so.

After reviewing the available experimental evidence, Fraleigh (1956) also identified a moderate relationship between physical activity and what he termed social adjustment, but he avoided the error of interpreting a cause and effect relationship. Fraleigh did suggest, however, that this relationship may be a spiraling circular one:

> . . . *the better-adjusted tend to participate in more social and competitive play because they have relatively higher levels of physical skill and because of their higher skill levels they gain favorable self-evaluations in addition to higher status recognition from their peer groups. On the other hand, the more poorly adjusted tend to participate in more individualized and less competitive play because of relatively lower levels of physical skill. This lower level of skill leaves the more poorly adjusted in a less advantageous position in terms of gaining desirable evaluations of self and high status recognition from the peer group.* [1956:271.]

How does one enter this circular relationship? One way may be to improve motor skills. Although the evidence is far from conclusive, several studies have shown that in some cases improvement in motor skills by participation in motor development programs or other forms of physical activity has resulted in increased peer acceptance and self-concept. (Buell et al.,

1968; Haley, 1969; Johnston et al., 1966.) Brown (1970), for example, determined that a six-week motor development program improved preschool males' ability to acquire rapport, to communicate, and to accept responsibility. The results failed to reveal significant increases in the ability to relate to other peers, but the improved ability to communicate and the increased ability to accept responsibility were significant outcomes of the motor development program.

The development of positive interpersonal competencies from participation in physical activity programs, of course, has not always been observed (Olson, 1968). Further research, however, giving careful attention to the type of physical activity, the instructional techniques used, and the specific interpersonal skills to be developed, should aid in clarifying these ambiguities.

CHANGING DIRECTIONS

Several developments must occur if we are to acquire a better understanding of the physical activity-interpersonal competence relationship. First we must obtain a better conception of precisely what is involved in the socialization process and what interpersonal competence is. In the latter case, for example, we may make use of the conceptual frame for interpersonal competence developed by Weinstein (1969). The most critical feature of interpersonal competence, according to Weinstein, is the skill in establishing and maintaining desired identities, both for one's self and for others. This skill is dependent upon three other variables:

1. *Empathy*—a person needs to be able to take the role of the other person accurately. The person must be able to predict the impact that various lines of action will have on another person.
2. The individual needs to acquire a large and varied *repertoire* of lines of action.
3. The person needs to possess certain *interpersonal resources* to be capable of employing tactics in appropriate situations.

The variables identified by Weinstein that are important in the development of interpersonal competence suggest that another development must take place in the physical activity-interpersonal competence relationship. We need to assess the influence of physical activities on more specific interpersonal skills rather than attempting to assess such broad concepts as social adjustment or social development by questionable measurement techniques.

For example, Argyle and Kendon (1967) have suggested that a social encounter between two persons is more or less a skilled social performance, analogous to a skilled motor performance. In a social encounter each person's performance is in part determined by his conception of the person with whom he is interacting. Thus one of the functions of the social performance is to convey the desired conception of yourself to the other person. Individuals vary markedly in this ability to present themselves as they wish to be perceived; that is, they differ in this particular interpersonal skill. A more specific question that we might ask is: Does participation in specific types of sports, for example, individual versus team sports, facilitate the ability to present one's self as desired? Hundreds of similar questions could and should be asked. The social technology necessary for assessing such aspects of an encounter as self-presentation in terms of verbal and nonverbal communication (proxemics) between social performers is now available.

We must also be concerned with how these specific interpersonal skills are acquired when involved in physical activity. There is an implicit learning model underlying what has been said about socialization and interpersonal competence. An extremely important role has been given to social learning. To understand how specific interpersonal skills are acquired we must observe how coaches affect their athletes, how physical educators affect their students, and how opponents affect each other through modeling and reinforcement procedures. In essence then, to know how interpersonal skills are acquired we must know how socialization agents use modeling and reinforcement methods when involved in physical activity.

Our conclusion then is clear. We have insufficient experimental evidence to warrant any generalization about the influence of physical activity on the development of interpersonal competence. Of course, this should not be interpreted to mean that participation in physical activities does not fulfill this socialization function in some way. However, as yet we have little knowledge of how the agents and agencies who use physical activities actually fulfill this function. And only when we understand how the development of interpersonal competence is achieved, will we be able to determine the extent to which the agencies who use physical activities contribute to the development of interpersonal competence.

Thus far our discussion of interpersonal competence has been in general terms and directed primarily at the development of behavioral skills. In subsequent chapters we continue to examine the relationship between physical activity and three of the more important social variables related not only to the development of interpersonal competence but to the development of a socially competent person.

CHAPTER 8 | AGGRESSION

Why do parents commit violence against their children? Why do nations go to war? Why do lovers hurt each other? Why does man attempt to destroy himself? The answers to these questions form the basis for some of the most significant yet perplexing problems in the study of man. Why people do horrific things to each other appears to be beyond rational explanation. The ubiquity of violence has made aggression a major concern of our society. In fact it would be safe to say that our greatest socialization problem is learning to control aggression. But some say man possesses an instinct for aggression—it is innate rather than learned behavior. Thus efforts to socialize man in order to control or eliminate his agressive behavior are of no avail. Instead, ethologists such as Lorenz (1966), Ardrey (1961, 1966), and Morris (1968) suggest that man must be provided with opportunities to discharge his instinctive aggressive tendencies through vigorous physical activity and competitive sports. Hence aggression researchers such as J. P. Scott (1970) have said that "violent exercise is nature's tranquilizer" (p. 20).

Other writers have also commented on the importance of physical activity and sports in the control of aggression. Smith states that:

When an individual is operating under stress he often becomes anxious and hypertense. One useful remedy for this situation is a heavy bout of physical exercise, which can restore the body to a state of physiological and psychological equilibrium. If the individual does not release this excess energy through a healthy outlet such as sport, it could be stored up and expressed later as hostile or violent behavior. [1971:47.]

And the noted ethologist Anthony Storr wrote:

Meanwhile it is obvious that the encouragement of competition in all possible fields is likely to diminish the kind of hostility which leads to war rather than to increase it . . . rivalry between nations in sport can do nothing but good. [1968:132.]

The belief that physical exercise and competitive sports relieve anxieties and tensions, that they provide a wholesome outlet for the expression of aggression arising from daily frustrations is widely accepted. But is sport itself not frustrating at times? Does competition not elicit anxiety and tension? In fact, under the stringent rules of many sports is there not less tolerance for antisocial behavior than in many other social situations? Although it would be highly desirable that sport serve as a "training ground for the control of aggression," as Scott (1970, p. 16) suggests, it is not at all clear how such training may come about. But the notion that sport serves such a purpose is intriguing and, as noted, a popular view. Consequently, we examine the role of sport in controlling aggression by using the same strategy of the previous chapters. First we will carefully define the aggression nomenclature and then examine the various theories and research on the antecedents of aggression and the control of aggression. And, finally, we will see what really is known about the role of sport and physical activity in the control of aggression.

AGGRESSION NOMENCLATURE

In everyday usage the term *aggression* is associated with attack or injury to some object. But a more rigorous definition of aggression is required in order that we can communicate with greater conceptual clarity. Dollard et al. (1939, p. 11) defined aggression as "a response having for its goal the injury of a living organism." But the rigor of this definition presents more problems than it solves. It is not possible to judge an act as aggressive only in terms of its effects on the victim, but we must consider the intentions and expectations on the part of the aggressor. Kaufmann's definition, states that for a behavioral act to be labeled aggressive:

1. *It must be transitive; that is, directed against a living target;*
2. *The attacker must have an expectation or subjective probability greater than zero of reaching the object and of imparting a noxious stimulus to it, or both.* [1970:10–11.]

To elaborate, harm to another person without intent (e.g., an accident) is not aggression. While dreams and fantasies have been called aggression, they are not considered aggression in the above definition. And of course inflicting hurt in order to help (e.g., a surgeon performing an appendectomy) is not aggression. On the other hand, although an aggressor fails to successfully inflict injury to another when he so intended, it is still by definition an aggressive act. Similarly aggression occurs even when the attacker aggresses under force or duress, as long as he knows that the resulting behavior will inflict harm.

In some situations no direct desire to injure a person exists.

Instead nonaggressive goals are sought, such as robbing a bank. But because the robber has a fair expectation that the robbery might result in injury, if injury occurs, it is aggression. Aggression occurring in the achievement of nonaggressive goals is known as *instrumental agression*. In contrast, aggression where the goal is injury to some object is known as *anger* or *reactive aggression*. Instrumental aggression is not a response to frustration and does not involve anger.

The term *anger* will be used to denote "a physiological arousal state coexisting with fantasied or intended acts culminating in harmful effects on another person" (Kaufmann, 1970, p. 12). But anger may occur without a person committing an act of aggression. Consequently a person may aggress without being angry, and he may be angry without aggressing.

The terms *violence* and *hostility* require definition to complete our semantic safari of the aggression nomenclature. *Violence* is similar to aggression, but connotes the more severe forms of physical aggression. *Hostility* is a personality characteristic or disposition. While aggression is a class of behaviors, hostility is a tendency to respond with a certain degree of aggression to particular stimuli. Aggressiveness is sometimes used interchangeably with hostility, but aggressiveness has come to convey a positive achievement-oriented disposition. Hostility conveys the negative connotation desired in referring to the tendency to aggress.

AGGRESSION THEORIES

Three major theories have been formulated to explain the occurrence of aggression in man: (1) the instinct theory, (2) the frustration-aggression hypothesis, and (3) the social learning theory.

Instinct Theory

The position that aggression is a biological instinct of man, and thus its expression is inevitable, has long been associated with Freud. More recently the instinct theory has received wide publicity through the writings of ethologists, best represented by Lorenz (1966) and Ardrey (1961, 1966). According to Lorenz the aggressive instinct has had important survival value in the evolution of man, but rapid technological changes have outstripped the slower evolution of innate inhibitions against the expression of aggression. Hence the inevitable expression of aggression must find periodic outlets, otherwise the innate drive to aggress would build up pressure inside the organism (like steam in an unregulated boiler) until it eventually burst into some form of violent behavior. Moreover, says Lorenz, the problem with modern society is that insufficient opportunities are provided for the discharge of a high aggressive drive. But it is precisely here where sport and vigorous physical activity have their value, says Lorenz. They provide man with an opportunity to "let off steam" in a wholesome way.

Instinct theorists have thus concluded that we should have more competitive sports, particularly sports that are vigorous and allow aggressive behavior, and that bigger and better olympic games should facilitate world peace. But as Kaufmann (1970) observes, "this prescription leads to the inference that people and nations engaged in competitive sports would be less aggressive than others. One is at a loss, however, to find even anecdotal evidence that such activities distinguish combative from peace-loving peoples" (p. 17).

The most disheartening aspect of the instinct theory is its forecast for the control of aggression. Because aggression must inevitably be expressed, our only hope is to channel it, but it can never be abolished. Most behavioral scientists have not been able to accept this bleak view of man. For this and other reasons, the instinct theory of aggression has been frequently aggressed against by hostile scientists.

These scientists' objections have not been that they deny possible innate tendencies, but that the instinct theory is a terminal position that accepts the nature of man as unchangeable. More importantly the evidence in support of the instinct theory is insufficient and refuted by a substantial body of recent aggression research. The objections to the instinct theory as espoused by Lorenz and other ethologists is summarized nicely by Berkowitz (1969b). "Their reliance on casual anecdotes instead of carefully controlled, systematic data, their use of ill-defined terms and gross analogies, and their disregard of hundreds of relevant studies in the interest of an oversimplified theory warrant the disapproval generally accorded them by technical journals" (p. 383).

Frustration-Aggression Hypothesis

The most widely recognized and influential theory of aggression states that aggression is always a consequence of frustration. Dollard et al. (1939) stated this position some 40 years ago saying the "occurrence of aggressive behavior always presupposes the existence of frustration and, contrariwise, the existence of frustration always leads to some form of aggression" (p. 11). The frustration-aggression (F-A) hypothesis was based on four major concepts: aggression, frustration, inhibition, and displacement. *Frustration* is a condition that exists when a goal response suffers interference. The amount of frustration is a function of the strength of instigation to the frustrated goal response, the degree of interference with the frustrated goal response, and the number of goal-response sequences frustrated. *Inhibition* is the tendency to restrain acts because of the anticipated negative consequences. *Displacement* is the tendency to engage in acts of aggression that are directed against some other target rather than at the source of the frustration.

Although space does not permit a detailed review of all the propositions of the F-A hypothesis, below are summarized some of the major ones:

1. The strength of instigation to aggression varies directly with the amount of frustration.
2. The strongest instigation aroused by frustration is to acts of aggression directed against the agent perceived to be the source of the frustration; progressively weaker instigations are aroused to progressively less direct acts of aggression.
3. The inhibition of any act of aggression varies directly with the strength of the punishment anticipated for its expression.
4. The inhibition of direct acts of aggression is an additional frustration that instigates aggression against the agent perceived to be responsible for this inhibition and increases

the instigation to other forms of aggression. Consequently a strong tendency exists for inhibited aggression to be displaced to different objects and expressed in modified forms.

Among the more popular hypotheses generated from the F-A hypothesis is the catharsis notion or cathartic effect. Catharsis, meaning literally a cleansing of the emotions, is the process or purging of drive or energy resulting in lessened arousal. The catharsis hypothesis states:

5. The expression of any act of aggression is a catharsis that reduces the instigation to all other acts of aggression.

Many other hypotheses can be generated from these basic propositions, and considerable research has concentrated on inhibition, object and response displacement, and the occurrence of catharsis. However the crucial problem of understanding the antecedent conditions giving rise to the F-A relationship has been ignored. The result has been attacks on the basic premise of the F-A hypothesis. Profound intelligence is not required to observe that people frequently suffer frustrations but do not inevitably aggress. The authors of the F-A hypothesis conceded this point and modified their position to state that aggression need not be observable, but could take the form of verbal, fantasied, or implied aggression.

Thus they argued that even though diluted or disguised, aggression was never destroyed. Aggression so defined is so protean that it has no scientific value. It is impossible to observe. And the same dilution destroyed the functional value of the concept frustration. Frustration was initially defined as an observable event, but under criticism the authors changed their position, describing it as an internal mechanism. Hence both frustration and aggression may be unobservable. Consequently when either frustration or aggression is observed the other is implied, which of course is a circular position having no functional use in explaining a cause and effect relationship.

An example illustrates: John has been frustrated because he is aggressing. Although I don't know how John was frustrated, I know he must have been; otherwise he would not have aggressed. And conversely: John has a desire to aggress because he was just frustrated. Although I cannot see any aggressive behavior, I know it is in John because he was frustrated. Because of the difficulty of knowing the sources of frustration, the F-A hypothesis has not been very satisfactory in predicting aggression. And then too some of the greatest atrocities are committed by individuals who appear to be no more frustrated than anyone else.

Social Learning Theory

Rather than frustration triggering some mechanism that inevitably manifests aggression, social learning theory postulates that aggression is a learned social behavior. Social learning theory places emphasis on the learning of aggression through the socialization process via vicarious or observational learning and social reinforcement. Thus social learning theorists argue that it is essential to examine the experiences of the aggressor, to know something about the victim or target of aggression, and to know something about the immediate circumstances of the aggressive situation. Having information about the aggressor, the victim, and the aggressive situation has been shown to be much more efficacious in predicting the frequency and intensity of aggression than the instinct theory of the F-A hypothesis.

Social learning research on aggression has focused largely on the influence of primary socialization agents, particularly parents, on how children learn aggressive behavior. Parents have been shown to be important models of aggression, and in general the literature confirms the common notion that parents who are aggressive have children who are aggressive. Obviously, other agents such as teachers and athletic coaches, are potentially important models in learning to act aggressively or nonaggressively. Although we have no specific evidence regarding the influence of teachers and coaches, considerable research has demonstrated that aggression is indeed learned by observing others aggress and the learning is not specific to a particular situation but is generalized.

As we would expect, reinforcement research has shown that when a person engages in aggression and is reinforced positively, the probability of aggression occurring under similar situations is increased. Continued positive reinforcement for certain agressive acts will eventually form a habit or tendency to respond to various stimuli with aggression. The observation and reinforcement of aggression over time then helps develop a high hostility personality disposition. Similarly the observation and reinforcement of nonaggression helps form a low hostility personality disposition.

Currently much research is being conducted on the situational determinants of aggression. Space does not permit coverage of this voluminous research, but the reader will find some help in Kaufmann (1970) and Berkowitz (1962, 1969a). Social learning theory has proven moderately successful in predicting aggression, particularly when we know something about both the aggressor and the immediate situation. This theory, contrary to the instinct theory and the F-A hypothesis, has proven potential for future research. But the theory has not gone uncriticized. These criticisms and an alternative position are considered next.

Berkowitz's Reformulation

The F-A hypothesis has been criticized for postulating that aggression is an innate response to frustration. Bandura and Walters (1963) have shown that learning can modify reactions to frustration, indicating that aggression is not the inevitable consequence. This had led some to conclude that because learning can modify the response to frustration, aggression cannot be innately determined, but is always learned. Berkowitz (1965) takes the position, however, that learning and innate determination of aggression can coexist in man. While man may have an innate predisposition to respond aggressively to frustration, this response can be modified by learning. (An innate predisposition should not be equated with an instinct; an instinct is not modifiable by learning.) Berkowitz's position then is that while frustration does not always lead to aggression, frustrating events increase the probability of the person aggressing soon afterward.

Aggression may not occur after frustration if (1) the person has learned a nonaggressive response to that situation and/or (2) the target has inappropriate stimulus qualities. Thus the F-A hypothesis should not be rejected on the basis that frustration does not result in aggression, for many times it certainly does, but that aggression is not an inevitable consequence of frustration.

As with all sciences, simple explanations initially are sought when studying some new phenomenon, but behavioral scientists inevitably have discovered that behavioral phenomena are not simply explained. And aggression is no exception. So far each theory has attributed the occurrence of aggression to one source; be it the consequence of an instinct, a response to frustration, or a learned response. Berkowitz's reformulated F-A hypothesis has suggested that learning can modify the response to frustration. But even in this reformulation, frustration is implied to be the sole source of aggression. Berkowitz (1969b) does not believe that only one source can account for all aggression. He not only argues cogently but documents his belief that aggression may occur for one or more of at least three reasons: (1) *frustration* of goal directed behavior, (2) *learning* aggressive behavior to certain stimuli, and (3) *pain*.

Although not discussed previously, pain has been shown to be a reliable cause of aggression. (Ulrich, 1966.) According to Berkowitz pain does not elicit aggression because it is frustrating, but because both pain and frustration are aversive stimuli that increase arousal. Heightened arousal in turn increases the probability of aggressive responses when certain environmental cues exist. For example, Berkowitz and LePage (1967) found that the presence of a rifle and pistol as compared to a neutral object resulted in stronger attacks upon a tormentor by provoked subjects. We will return to the issue of arousal and environmental cues when discussing the relationship between aggression and sport.

In summary, the most plausible view of aggression today is that while aggression may have some innate determinants, these determinants may be modified through learning. Aggression is not inevitable in man; he can learn not to aggress just as he can learn to aggress.

AGGRESSION AND SPORT

At least two major questions can be raised about the relationship between aggression and sport or general physical activity. First, how do we control violence in sport? And second, does sport or physical activity control, reduce, or eliminate aggression? Our emphasis here shall be on answering the latter question because the former is ultimately answered in the latter.

The theoretical positions reviewed above suggest quite different relationships between sport and aggression. According to the instinct theory man must have some opportunity to express his inevitable aggressive behavior. Thus instinct theory prescribes sport as a mild aggressive activity to reduce aggressive instigation. On the other hand, social learning theorists would argue that if aggression in sport is positively reinforced, it will strengthen aggressive habits while decreasing inhibitions against aggression.

The notion that sport may eliminate wars and reduce violent crimes is appealing when attempting to justify large expenditures on athletic programs, but requires proof when proposed to behavioral scientists and critical thinking students. Just as the instinct theory has not proven to be a viable explanation of aggressive behavior, its recommendation that sport is an outlet for aggression may be discounted as too simplistic. Thus in the following section we shall only consider the social learning position and the revised F-A hypothesis when examining the empirical research surrounding the relationship between sport and aggression. This relationship will be examined through two issues, the cathartic effect and competition.

Cathartic Effect

The notion that acts of aggression will reduce the incidence of further aggression has prima facie plausibility. Freud and other psychoanalytic theorists have placed considerable emphasis on the cathartic effect, frequently using this notion to explain man's *need* to purge himself of aggressive tendencies. But what does experimental research indicate about the catharsis hypothesis in general, and have we any evidence that sport or vigorous physical activity has a cathartic effect?

The general experimental research that has tested the catharsis hypothesis indicates that aggressive behavior results in less subsequent aggression in some instances, and more aggression in others. (Kaufmann, 1970.) One hypothesis for reconciling these differences is that catharsis does not occur when *instru-mental* aggression is committed, but that *anger* or *reactive* aggression is cathartic. Although this hypothesis has received some support, more frequently it has not been substantiated. Several in-depth reviews of the catharsis hypothesis literature have concluded that it has little basis in fact and that social learning theory can better predict the occurrence of aggression. (Nighswander and Mayer, 1969; Berkowitz, 1962; Buss, 1961.)

Unfortunately the role of sport or physical activity as a cathartic agent has never been clearly delineated. It is obscure whether all sports or only those that provide some latitude for aggression possess cathartic qualities. Intuitively it would seem unlikely that all sports possess some mystical quality that elim-inates aggressive tendencies. Also it is unclear whether catharsis is the consequence of actually committing aggression when par-ticipating in sports or whether it results merely from engaging in vigorous physical activity.

Assuming for a moment that catharsis occurs as a result of the actual expression of aggression, does sport provide greater opportunity and tolerance for being violent? The answer prob-ably is dependent upon which sport we consider. Certainly non-contact sports provide little special opportunity to aggress. But in most contact sports, stringent rules usually enforced by offi-cials who carefully scrutinize players' behaviors, place heavy penalties, including ejection from the contest, for committing aggression. Thus if the cathartic effect is a consequence of com-mitting aggression, sport in general appears to tolerate no more, if not less, actual aggression than other segments of society. Hence the notion that sport is a panacea for the control of violence because it offers an opportunity for the mild expression of aggression is questionable. Moreover, even when aggression occurs in sport we have no experimental verification that it has cathartic value.

Some may take issue with the assertion that in sport aggres-sion or violence is not tolerated. They may argue that all we need to do is watch a professional football or hockey game and we will witness plenty of aggression. But it is precisely at this point that we encounter semantic confusion about the meaning of aggression. All too often aggression is equated with vigorous physical activity in contact sports. If a player plays aggressively (meaning with high motivation), he is soon called aggressive and many of his acts done with intense physical effort are interpreted as acts of aggression. An aggressive player (high motivation) who plays aggressively is mistakenly considered to be committing aggression. Even when injury to player A occurs as an accident of player B's aggressive (high motivation) behavior it is not by definition aggression. Player B must have an *intent* to hurt player A. Of course it is often very difficult to determine intent, but in almost every sport officials are given the responsibility to do so. And when an official believes that a player intended harm, severe penalties are usually invoked. Thus it appears debatable that sport is a convenient and useful institution of society for allowing, or perhaps encouraging aggression and acts of violence. Instead sport usually is carefully policed, providing an opportunity to pursue nonharmful goals with intensity through vigorous physical activity.

Perhaps then the cathartic effect is primarily the outcome of the vigorous physical activity associated with some sports. Actually, according to the F-A hypothesis, only previous acts of aggression were considered cathartic, but in its broader usage, the cathartic effect refers to any agent that reduces aggressive tendencies. Therefore, we now examine the question: Does vigorous physical activity have a cathartic effect?

Ryan (1970) experimentally investigated this question by angering subjects through the use of an obnoxious behaving accomplice. One group of angered subjects was required to pound ten times on a device with a large mallet and another group was required to sit quietly. Then half of each group were given the opportunity to first shock the accomplice and then an innocent bystander, and the other half were given the same opportunity but in reverse order. The results showed that the pounding activity had no cathartic effect; that is, it did not lessen the aggressive tendencies of the subjects. Ryan also found that when angered, the most effective means to reduce aggressive tendencies is to retaliate against the anger instigator.

Although Ryan's study suggests that physical activity is not cathartic, perhaps pounding a mallet ten times was not sufficiently vigorous. Unfortunately, little help is available from the remaining experimental literature. These studies have examined the influence of participating in vigorous physical sports, such as football and wrestling, on the reduction of aggressive tendencies, but have found ambiguous results. Almost all of these studies have suffered from methodological problems, most notedly the use of personality measures of aggressiveness (not hostility) as a measure of aggression. Both Ryan (1970) and Layman (1970) conclude from reviewing the catharsis literature related to physical activity, that the catharsis hypothesis is unsubstantiated experimentally.

Rather than vigorous physical activity decreasing subsequent aggression, some recent evidence suggests that increased physical activity may make an individual more susceptible to aggression when confronted with potential aggressive stimuli. Zillmann et al. (1972) conducted an experiment in which half of the subjects were highly aroused by means of strenuous physical exercise and the other half of the subjects were in a low arousal condition. The highly aroused subjects, when angered by an accomplice, administered much more intense shock to the accomplice than subjects who were low in arousal and angered. Zillmann et al. conclude that "the findings are clearly counter to the explanation that strenuous physical exercise . . . can serve to drain aggressive tensions and thus induce catharsis" (as long as the person does not reach a state of acute exhaustion). The increased physical activity is viewed as residual activation which, when present at the time of aggressive instigation, greatly facilitates aggressive responses. This is the result of the person attributing his arousal to the environmental cues present, which thus intensify the emotion to which the cues are cognitively associated. We will make additional reference to this point later.

Another question relevant to sports activities is whether the observation of violence in sports is cathartic or conducive to more violence. Walters (1966) cites considerable evidence that the observation of violence has no cathartic effect but in fact increases the likelihood of aggression through observational learning. Thus if much violence is observed in sports, it seems likely that instead of curbing spectator violence, it will heighten aggression tendencies. It is not an uncommon observation that when violence has occurred among spectators it has frequently been preceded by violence among the players.

In conclusion, there is little empirical basis for the catharsis hypothesis in general or for sport specifically. It remains a mystery why the catharsis hypothesis has had such popular appeal when receiving virtually no scientific support. The expression of aggression subsequent to previous aggression or physical activity will more likely be determined by the rewards or punishments received for the initial aggressive act and by learned situational determinants. Moreover we have no support for the idea that vicarious participation in aggression reduces subsequent aggression. And as Bandura (1965) has noted, ". . . advocates of the catharsis hypothesis rarely recommend vicarious participation in sexual activities as a means of reducing sexual behaviors" (p. 326).

Competition
Caplow (1964) wrote: "In virtually all competitive situations some degree of hostility develops between the competitors . . ." (p. 318). Caplow fails to substantiate this claim, but perhaps a touch of truth can be found in this statement. Sports by definition are competitive, and competition is potentially quite frustrating. Recall that frustration occurs when a goal response suffers interference. In competition each competitor is clearly interfering with the other's goal response. Both cannot be victorious and defeat frequently results in loss of self-esteem. Feshbach (1971) has stated that probably the most important source of anger and resultant aggression is a result of violations to self-esteem through insult or humiliation. Thus competition is a frequent source of frustration and frustration increases the likelihood of aggression. Social learning theorists have recognized this for some time, frequently using competitive situations to manipulate frustration in order to observe aggressive tendencies.

Thus the question is: Does competition increase aggression? Potentially it appears yes, but does it in actuality? A field experiment by Muzafer and Carolyn Sherif (1953) provides us with insight into the compelling role of competitive sports on aggression. This study was carried out in a summer camp for boys and involved three stages. In stage one, boys were given maximum freedom to participate in campwide activities through informal groups. In stage two, two teams were formed in which all camp activities were done separately. In stage three, the Sherifs wanted to study intergroup relations, so they presented the teams with a series of competitive games and also arranged some frustrating situations for each team. In stages one and two, aggression was very infrequent, but the competition among the two teams in stage three resulted in considerable aggression. In fact violence became so recurrent between the two groups that the camp counselors had to take steps to restore harmony before anyone was injured. This was accomplished by breaking up the teams and by initiating competition with a nearby camp. Two additional points about this study merit mention. First, while the losers of the contests were prone to initiate aggression after the activity, both the losers and winners were quick to resort to aggression and counter-aggression during the activity when frustrated. Second, although competition appears to have provoked aggression among the boys in the camp, other factors were operative in the competitive situation. Thus a closer inspection of the competitive situation is needed.

An important factor within a competitive situation is whether a person is defeated or victorious. Among the more obvious hypotheses about the influence of competition on aggression is that defeat will instigate greater aggressive tendencies than victory. Ryan (1970) tested this hypothesis among some subjects who were angered previously and some who were not. Regardless of the presence or absence of anger, subjects who were victorious in competition were less aggressive than subjects who lost. Ryan suggests that rather than competition itself being frustrating, it is the outcome of the competition that determines frustration. Of course, events during competition can also be frustrating and increase the probability of aggression.

Several other hypotheses that appear logical from the revised F-A hypothesis are: (1) Frustration is greater when a player loses to a near-equally matched opponent. A person who sees no opportunity for victory is less frustrated than a person who has victory within his grasp but loses it. (2) The more significant the rewards or outcomes associated with winning the greater the frustration when losing. Thus the probability of aggression is higher when the contest is close and the rewards are high. These hypotheses need testing and both sport and laboratory settings are conducive to their empirical analysis.

In sport, competition between two persons provides not only the opportunity for aggression by one opponent, but counter-aggression by the other opponent. Indeed many aggressive acts are retaliations to an attack. A recent series of studies has investigated the influence of the degree of defeat, the opponent's intended level of aggression, and the actual influence of a competitive situation on a person's counter-aggression. These studies had subjects compete in a reaction time task in which the loser received a shock of an intensity set by the winner. Subjects always determined the intensity of shock before the trial began and received feedback about the intensity level of shock set by his opponent after the trial regardless of winning or losing.

Studies by Epstein and Taylor (1967) and Shortell et al. (1970) found that the degree of defeat or victory had no effect on counter-aggression. This appears inconsistent with the findings of Sherif and Sherif (1953) and Ryan (1970), although the Sherif and Ryan studies were not primarily interested in counter-aggression. These counter-aggression studies revealed that defeat was frustrating, but it had no effect on anger, and generally only produced feelings of disappointment. The intensity of counter-aggression, however, was directly related to the subject's perception of the aggressive intent of the opponent (the intensity of the shock administered by the opponent). Increased aggressive retaliation was prompted by increased aggressive intent when competing. Taylor and Epstein (1967) also found that males reacted aggressively to provocation by male opponents but unaggressively to female opponents. Females, on the other hand, were unaggressive to female opponents but reacted to provocation by male opponents in a highly aggressive manner.

While it is clear that attack is a potent source for eliciting aggression, it still remains unclear whether competition itself elicits aggression. Gaebelein and Taylor (1971) in two studies found that various levels of competition under controlled levels of attack did not influence aggression. Instead they suggest that competition, like frustration, only increases a person's readiness to respond in an aggressive manner. It requires other situational factors or stimuli, such as an intended aggressive attack, to provoke a person to aggression.

An underlying theme linking what may appear to be unrelated findings emerges in this chapter through the concept of "undifferentiated arousal." Substantial evidence indicates that arousal which is unassociated with a particular emotion or stimulus will be labeled according to available environmental stimuli. This has led aggression researchers, notably Berkowitz (1969a), to the position that undifferentiated arousal, when present in a situation that has environmental cues suggesting aggression, will intensify the aggressive response. For example, Geen and O'Neal (1969) found that undifferentiated arousal resulted in more aggression by persons who saw an aggressive boxing film than by individuals who saw the film but were not aroused. Earlier we mentioned that Berkowitz and LePage (1967) found that the visual presence of aggressive stimuli (a rifle and pistol) elicited more aggression among aroused subjects. And finally Zillmann et al. (1972) observed that the heightened arousal resulting from vigorous physical activity, when associated with aggressive environmental cues, increased the probability of aggression. And now, from the evidence pertaining to the influence of competition on aggression, we at least have the suggestion of a similar theme. Competition is a source of frustration and frustration engenders arousal. Does this heightened arousal that is manifested by competition also increase the probability of aggression when associated with aggressive environmental cues? From Gaebelein and Taylor (1971) we may infer that the answer is yes, but of course we must wait until the question is directly investigated before speculating further.

CONCLUSION

Perhaps sport or physical activity may help in controlling aggression but it is not a catharsis, nor does it provide relief for instinctively generated tensions or excess energy. Aggression is behavior not simply determined, but is the result of frustration, pain, and learned responses. We can better predict the occurrence of aggression by knowing something about the aggressor, the victim, and the immediate situation. Sport or physical activity is not some mystical panacea that reduces aggressive tendencies or serves as an outlet for the expression of aggression. We must critically inspect these activities to understand their potential not only for controlling aggression but for eliciting aggression.

In this chapter we have attempted to explode some of the myths concerning the relationship between sport, physical activity, and aggression. It is clear that competitive sports have inherent stimulus qualities that make them frustrating, and hence a potential source of aggression. But behavioral research also shows that individuals can learn nonaggressive responses to aggressive situations. Learning occurs largely by observing others and by being reinforced positively for appropriate responses and negatively for inappropriate responses. Thus the implications are clear. Persons who observe violence and are reinforced for violence when participating in sports are likely to continue violent behavior. When individuals observe nonviolent behavior and are reinforced for nonviolent behavior they are likely to continue to behave nonviolently.

CHAPTER 9 | ATTITUDES

The study of attitudes has been among the more popular research topics in physical education, primarily for the wrong reasons. First, it has been a common belief that attitude research was easy to conduct and second that the mere assessment of individual attitudes toward some aspect of physical education or sport had important practical implications. The first is definitely untrue, for attitude research is a highly complex and difficult task when done correctly. Because the vast quantity of attitude research in physical education has largely ignored developments in attitude theory and measurement, the second is also untrue. Moreover, physical education attitude research has shown little concern for determining how attitudes are formed or how they may be changed. Although there may be some immediate practical value in knowing people's attitudes toward many aspects of physical education, the more important concern is with how these attitudes are formed, how they can be changed, and how these attitudes actually affect behavior.

One important function of society's socialization agents is to teach or transmit desirable attitudes. Thus in this chapter we will begin by acquiring an appreciation of the complexity of attitudes and their assessment. We then will consider some of the key components in attitude formation and change. We will determine what is known about attitudes toward physical activity, sport, sportsmanship, and other factors of interest to physical educators. And we will consider the role that physical activity may play in attitude formation, particularly the attitude one has of himself or his self-concept.

WHAT IS AN ATTITUDE?

In 1935 Allport defined an attitude as "a mental and neural state of readiness, organized through experience, exerting a directive or dynamic influence upon the individual's response to all objects and situations with which it is related" (p. 805). More recently Triandis (1971) has defined an attitude as "an idea charged with emotion which predisposes a class of actions to a particular class of social situations" (p. 2). The common element in each of these definitions and in most other definitions of attitude is the "readiness to respond" or "predisposition" toward a situation. In addition, attitudes are considered to be enduring but changeable, general rather than specific, and learned rather than innate.

To understand how attitudes relate to behavior three interrelated components of attitudes need to be distinguished: (1) a *cognitive* component that is conceptualized as a person's belief, ideas, or factual knowledge of some object or person. Assessing the cognitive component involves determining how an individual categorizes the stimuli associated with a particular attitude; (2) an *affective* component that is the person's evaluation of, liking of, or emotional response to some object or person; and

(3) a *behavioral* component that consists of the person's behavioral intention toward an object or person.

The enormous interest in attitudes as an area of study is not without reason. Attitudes serve an important function by helping us adjust to our complex environment, to protect our ego or self-esteem by allowing us to avoid unpleasant truths about ourselves, to express our values, and to help us understand our world. In early attitude research, a distinction was made between mental attitudes and motor attitudes, the latter referring to muscular preparation or set. This distinction is now passé because of its suggested mind-body dualism. Instead today an attitude implies both a mental aptness and a motor set.

One of the characteristics of an attitude is a consistent response to social situations; that is, from consistencies in thinking, feeling, and acting we infer the existence of an attitude. Because attitudes are characterized as being consistent, they are commonly thought to have a strong relationship to behavior. For example, if Fred Flaccid indicates that he is aware of the importance of physical exercise for maintaining good health, that good health is something he desires, and that he intends to participate in a daily physical exercise program, what are the chances that he in fact will exercise? If this is all that we know about Fred, the probability that he will exercise is not good. The relationship between attitude and behavior is rather weak; to predict behavior more accurately other factors must be known. Triandis explains:

> *What should be understood is this: Attitudes involve what people think about, feel about, and how they would like to behave toward an attitude object. Behavior is not only determined by what people would like to do but also by what they think they should do, that is, social norms, by what they have usually done, that is, habits, and by the* expected consequences of the behavior. [1971:14.]

To predict more accurately whether Fred Flaccid will in fact exercise regularly, besides knowing that he has a favorable attitude toward physical exercise, we need to know what he thinks he *should* do (norms). Does he have time for the exercise?

What does he think his neighbors or friends will think when they see him jogging around the block? Also we can more accurately predict his exercise behavior if we know how frequently and consistently he has exercised in the past (habits). And lastly we can increase our precision in predicting his behavior if we know what he thinks he will obtain from exercising and how important these outcomes are to him (expectations of reinforcement).

HOW ARE ATTITUDES MEASURED?

The measurement of attitudes has seen considerable progress over the last 50 years. Although some difference of opinion prevails, the separate measurement of each of the three components of an attitude is advocated by most attitude researchers today. In the past only the affective component usually has been measured.

Measurement of the Cognitive Component

You will recall that the cognitive component is concerned with how an individual categorizes the stimuli in his environment. In measuring the cognitive component the main task is to determine what categories the subject used to view a particular attitude object or some aspects of his experiences. For example, what are some categories you may use to think about sport? You may think in terms of the type of sport: individual versus team, contact versus noncontact, or self-paced versus reactive. Or you may categorize your thinking to such concepts as functional and nonfunctional, expressive and nonexpressive, participant and spectator.

Methods for assessing the cognitive component include the use of self-ratings of beliefs and the amount of knowledge about some attitude object. Statistical procedures such as factor analysis have been used to identify the group of stimuli that individuals associate with some attitude object. Another way to assess the cognitive component involves the elicitation of associations produced by the attitude object. This procedure involves the presentation of a series of stimuli to which the individual indicates the degree of association of each stimulus with the attitude object.

Measurement of the Affective Component

Here the measurement objective is to assess the degree of positive or negative affect associated with an attitude object. Physiological measures, usually of the autonomic nervous system, are the most direct procedures for measuring the affective component. Heart responses, galvanic skin response (GSR), and palmar sweat measures are examples of such measures. These methods are slow and time consuming and thus are not widely used. Instead standardized verbal scales are frequently used to measure the degree of positive or negative affect. These scales are best known to the individual casually acquainted with attitude measurement; they include both specific and general verbal methods. These classic methods have been reviewed by Edwards (1957), and include those scales developed by Thurstone (1928), Likert (1932), Guttman (1944), and Edwards and Kilpatrick (1948). Each of these scales is based on different scales of measurement (nominal, ordinal, equal interval), but has in common the use of verbal statements, which are anything that can be said about an attitude object.

These verbal attitude scales are constructed to measure the individual's affect toward a specific attitude object. Thus a different scale must be constructed using different items for each attitude object to be measured. Because there are thousands of attitude objects of interest, this method is inefficient and expensive. Thus the Semantic Differential (Osgood et al., 1957) has gained wide popularity as a general method for measuring any attitude object. In this method an attitude object is presented and subjects respond on a series of scales bound by polar adjectives. For example:

THE OLYMPIC GAMES
Good __:__:__:__:__:__:__ Bad
Strong __:__:__:__:__:__:__ Weak
Necessary __:__:__:__:__:__:__ Unnecessary

Measurement of the Behavioral Component

Two approaches have been used to measure the behavioral component: (1) direct observation of behavior and (2) the use of a verbal scale. Recall that the behavioral component is concerned with the *behavioral intentions* of an individual toward an attitude object. In the first approach inferences are made from observations of the consistencies in a person's behavior in response to common situations. This approach has weaknesses, however, as behavior is determined only in part by attitudes, and in part by norms, habits, and expectations of reinforcement. To measure the behavioral component of an attitude by observation of behavior the influence of these variables must be controlled, which is no easy task.

The second approach relies on verbal responses of a person toward some attitude object. For example, Triandis (1964) has developed the Behavioral Differential "which is a general instrument that measures the behavioral intentions of subjects toward any person or category of persons." For example:

MY HIGH SCHOOL FOOTBALL COACH

I would ___:___:___:___:___:___:___ I would not
obey this person

I would not ___:___:___:___:___:___:___ I would
ask this person for advice

I would ___:___:___:___:___:___:___ I would not
invite this person to dinner

A Final Comment on Measurement

We have only skimmed the surface of attitude measurement, and have ignored the issue of sampling, of subjects distorting their responses (social desirability), and other response biases. Another problem is that the direct methods of attitude measurement are quite transparent. The respondent knows what information is being sought. Fortunately, the semantic differential, which is becoming very popular, is less transparent because it usually is presented as a method for measuring the meaning of words. For a thorough review of other available indirect methods, see Campbell (1950).

ATTITUDE RESEARCH
IN PHYSICAL EDUCATION

Attitude is an attractive concept in physical education because it reflects an individual's previous experiences with particular attitude objects associated with physical education. Thus physical educators have been measuring attitudes formally and informally for some time. We often ask students or athletes their opinion on some aspect of physical education. An *opinion* is simply the verbal expression of an attitude, but an attitude can be expressed nonverbally as well. Unfortunately physical educators have restricted themselves to the measurement of verbal attitudes, and have ignored the measurement of nonverbally expressed attitudes. Hopefully, in future years, the study of nonverbal attitudes as expressed in human movement and their association with behavior (both physical and social) will receive attention. All of us have inferred attitudes about individuals by observing how they walk, their posture, gestures, and other movements.

Measuring Attitudes in Physical Education

The assessment of attitudes in physical education has paralleled the methods used in social psychology, but with a considerable time lag. When the Thurstone and Likert techniques were being used in the 1930s, physical educators were subjectively compiling questions to form an inventory without using any scaling methods. In the late 1940s and early 1950s, and continuing today, physical educators have been using the Likert and Thurstone methods. Although these techniques are still quite acceptable for certain assessment problems, social psychologists during this period began using the Guttman (1944) and Edwards and Kilpatrick (1948) methods with their superior scaling properties. Then in the 1960s and 1970s the assessment of the cognitive, affective, and behavioral components was developed by social psychologists. Additionally, the use of the semantic differential became common because of its superior characteristics. Recognition of the three components of an attitude and the need to assess each of these components, however, has not occurred in the physical education literature with one exception. Moreover the semantic differential has, to date, been used infrequently in physical education attitude research.

The best known and most frequently used standardized attitude scale in physical education is the Wear Attitude Inventory for Physical Education (1951, 1955). The scale, which has two equivalent forms, is a Likert-type scale and is designed to measure the direction and intensity of individual attitudes toward

physical education as an activity course. As with any standardized psychological instrument, the Wear Inventory has been
used both consistently and inconsistently in its initial purpose.

A number of other attitude scales have been developed and
published in the physical education literature. Each of these
scales has used a Thurstonian or Likert method, with few exceptions. These scales have been concerned largely with assessing
attitudes toward (1) physical education as a profession, (2)
physical activity, including exercise and fitness, (3) attitudes
toward competition and athletics in general, and (4) attitudes
toward sportsmanship.

What have we learned from these studies assessing attitudes
toward some aspect of physical education? In general we have
found that attitudes are largely positive, but sometimes not to
the desired extent. When assessing attitudes about the profession, physical educators have usually measured current profes-
sionals or students preparing to enter the profession. It would
be startling to learn that these individuals did not have positive
attitudes toward their chosen profession. No attempt has been
made to assess and report the attitudes of those outside our
profession toward physical education. Several sources, however,
indicate that physical education as a profession is not deemed
especially positive. When evaluating departments in terms of
academic prestige or scholarly importance, physical education is
usually quite low. As an occupation, an educator does not rank
very high, and among educators, a physical educator has even
less status.

Probably the most frequently assessed attitude has been
toward physical education as a general activity course in high
school and college. The results have almost always been positive,
with certain groups of individuals in some studies being more
positive than others. For example, athletes, students from small
high schools, students from farms, students selecting teaching
as a career, and those above average in skills have more positive
attitudes than their counterparts. (Mista, 1968; Brumbach and
Cross, 1965.) One interesting finding came from a study by
Keogh (1962), who reported that students endorsed the social,
physical and emotional values of physical education, but not
the relative value of a physical education program in the school

curriculum. Perhaps this suggests that students "like our product, but don't like the way it's packaged."

While athletics have always been popular in this country, they also have been subject to considerable debate regarding their overall value. For example, Bonzan (1965) used a Likert-type attitude scale to determine the attitudes of university publics toward the contributions of intercollegiate sports programs to general education. The general attitude was favorable, especially among alumni, undergraduates, and graduate students, but the faculty attitude was slightly unfavorable. Among freshman college males, Stubbs (1957) found their attitude toward athletics was quite favorable, but their attitude toward athletes was only slightly favorable. Among senior college males, however, Sheehan (1956) found that these students had positive attitudes toward athletics, the athletes, and the coaches. One must wonder how much these attitudes were influenced by the success or failure of the university athletic program for that particular season.

Within athletics a popular issue has been the desirability of competition, particularly intense competition, among women and elementary school children. Scott (1953) assessed the attitude of parents, teachers, and administrators toward intense competition among elementary school children. The results of her study showed that although there was a wide variation in opinion, the majority of the three groups were favorable toward intense competition at the elementary level with the parents being most favorable.

With respect to attitudes toward intense competition for women, Harres (1968) found that the general attitude was positive, but again there was a wide diversity in opinion. McGee (1956) found that administrators and teachers were much less favorable toward intensive competition for high school girls than were parents and coaches. More recently the issue of females having equal opportunities to compete, either in separate sports programs or in direct competition with males, is not only one of considerable attitudinal differences but in several instances has become an issue that has required litigation. In the immediate future it will be interesting to observe how attitudes change among different groups of individuals toward women competing in sports. It may be even more interesting and more useful to know *why* these attitudes change, if indeed they do.

Sportsmanship as an attitude has been of some interest to physical educators. McAfee (1955) gave a "home-made," non-scaled sportsmanship inventory to 6th, 7th, and 8th grade boys. The results indicated that the attitude toward sportsmanship became poorer with age. Both Kistler (1957) and Richardson (1962) found attitudes toward sportsmanship to be less than desirable among college-age students. Lakie (1964), in determining the extent to which athletes from different sports and types of schools differed in the win-at-any-cost philosophy, found no differences. The major problem with these studies, however, is that they have used unvalidated scales. That is, our society is not in consensus on many facets of what constitutes sportsmanlike behavior. For example, is it unsportsmanlike behavior not to tell the referee when you violated a rule that he did not see? To assess sportsmanship attitudes and evaluate them as positive or negative requires some process of confirming that the attitude is indeed in accord with or counter to prevailing acceptable behavior. This is a difficult if not an impossible task.

The attitude research reviewed thus far has been completely applied. That is, these studies sought to discover how individuals viewed certain issues at some particular time and if some individuals viewed some attitude object or event differently than others. The research has been atheoretical, making it impossible to reach any generalizations about the results that will predict attitude formation, attitude change, or the relation between attitude and behavior. Individual attitudes toward competition in 1955 have little significance today if we do not understand how the attitudes were formed or changed. For example, assessing attitudes about sex and smoking in 1955 would tell us little about our attitudes toward these things today. To ask broad questions such as what is your attitude toward physical activity, is not very fruitful either. Physical activity is a very broad concept with important components. To understand one's attitude toward physical activity and how this attitude was formed or can be changed, we need to understand how each component is viewed by our sample.

Kenyon (1968) has made a significant development in attitude research in physical education by conceptualizing physical activity on six dimensions. These dimensions were not figments of the imagination but were based on empirical research. Six dimensions were identified, including: physical activity for social purposes, health and fitness, thrills and excitement, aesthetic experience, recreation and relaxation, and to meet a physical challenge. Scales were then developed for assessing each of these dimensions. Although further development is suggested by Kenyon and appears warranted, this approach is superior to the generalized assessment of an attitude.

To use Kenyon's scales, however, merely to compile a library of facts about various groups of individuals' attitudes toward physical activity will not be useful. Instead we must reemphasize the position that the important function of studying attitudes is to learn how these attitudes are formed, how they may be changed, and how they relate to actual behavior. While Kenyon's attitude research with physical activity helps to delineate this attitude object, it will require the user of this instrument to place it into a theoretical structure.

Space does not allow us to review the many theories available to the student interested in attitude research. Suffice it to say, though, that social psychologists engaged in attitude research have not been "flying by the seat of their pants." Instead the emphasis in attitude research today has been toward the development of theory leading to an understanding of the determinants of attitudes, and once attitudes have been formed, how they can be changed.

One theory, however, warrants mention because of its wide recognition and extensive influence on attitude research in the recent past. The theory is Festinger's (1957) cognitive dissonance theory, which postulates that man has a desire to be consistent within himself, and that the presence of inconsistency or dissonance, as Festinger calls it, is psychologically uncomfortable. Dissonance may arise from new events or information, or from being confronted with alternative decisions in everyday situations. Because dissonance is an uncomfortable state, it will motivate the person to try to reduce the dissonance and achieve consonance. Festinger also hypothesizes that when dissonance is present the person will attempt to avoid situations and information that will likely increase the dissonance. The theory then elaborates on more specific ways that a person may attempt to reduce dissonance. The theory has received considerable experimental attention, being supported in part, refuted in part, but mostly elaborated upon or qualified since its initial formulation.

ATTITUDE FORMATION AND CHANGE

What are the factors that determine the formation of a particular attitude? In answering this question we will consider the formation of each of the three components of attitude. The cognitive component involves categorization of events occurring in our environment. That is, events with similar properties are placed into a category and we respond to those events in that category in a similar way. This helps simplify our world, but has the disadvantage of increasing the probability of perceiving events incorrectly. One frequent tendency is to "type" people and groups by overgeneralizing or oversimplifying our categories. This is known as *stereotyping*. A frequent stereotype in our society is with respect to football players. Some tend to think of all football players as muscle-bound, mesomorphic morons. The development of the cognitive component involves learning the category (football player), associating the category with other categories (mesomorphic people, or stupid) and evaluating the category (negative emotion).

The affective component is formed by association of physiological responses with certain cognitions. That is, we experience joy when arousal is manifested and the attitude object cognitively is interpreted to be desirable. We can experience the same arousal but cognitively interpret the object to be undesirable, experiencing anger. These associations are developed by conditioning the attitude object with rewards and aversive stimuli. The other factor helping to form the affective component of attitudes is the frequency of exposure to the object. In general, the more we are exposed to an object the more we like it, up to a point. Too much exposure, however, can decrease the attractiveness of an attitude object.

The behavioral component is largely determined by social norms or the ideas held by a group of people concerning what is appropriate and inappropriate behavior. In considering the development of the three components and their interrelations, Triandis writes:

We learn our attitudes either from direct experience or from other people. Direct experience is most relevant to the development of the cognitive and the affective components; other people (family and friends) are most relevant to the behavioral component. Of course, direct experience can have some implications for the behavioral component, because the three components interact and there is a tendency for them to become as consistent as possible. Conversely, other people can tell us not only how we should behave, thus influencing our behavioral component, but also how we should think and how we should feel about various attitude objects. On the other hand they cannot impose their views, although our parents make an attempt to tell us how to think and feel, we often develop our own ways of thinking and feeling. Nevertheless when they tell us how to behave they can also provide sanctions that will discourage us from deviations from these norms. [1971:119.]

How can attitudes be changed? Attitudes can be changed by modifying any of the three components. Because there is a tendency for the components to be consistent, a change in one will be reflected in changes in the other components. The cognitive component can be changed with new information (e.g., propaganda), the affective component can be changed by pleasant or unpleasant experiences in the presence of the attitude object, and the behavioral component can be modified by changes in norms (such as those associated with long hair styles for men) or by legal legislation (such as in civil rights issues). Also attitudes will often become consistent with events that have happened previously.

When considering attitude formation and change, two studies in physical education warrant discussion. Sheehan (1965) constructed what he called a "teaching model" for attitude formation and change through a physical education activity course. Based on his review of the attitude literature, he employed instructional procedures that initially effected the cognitive component, and subsequently the behavioral and affective components. The student attitude toward cooperation in team soccer play was the target. Sheehan showed that through purposeful, directed instruction toward cooperative attitudes, that indeed such attitudes could be modified. However, in another group who participated but did not have this purposeful instruction, no change in attitude toward cooperation was observed in the course. This study suggests that mere participation in a physical education activity class was not sufficient to alter one's attitude about cooperation, but through information and structured activity an attitude may be changed.

In an interesting study by Al-Talib (1970), the effect of playing a role consistent or inconsistent with one's attitude toward physical education was examined. Based on Festinger's dissonance theory, the study supported the hypothesis that playing a role favorable or unfavorable to an attitudinal object would result in an attitude change in the direction of the role played. That is, individuals with a positive attitude toward physical education, and role-played a negative attitude, changed to a less positive attitude. And for individuals who played a positive role, their positive attitude was strengthened.

SELF-CONCEPT:
AN ATTITUDE ABOUT THE SELF
Self-concept is not a single concept, but instead is a system of conceptions about oneself. In part it is an attitude about oneself. Similar to other attitudes, self-attitude has a cognitive, affective, and behavioral component. The cognitive component includes the categories a person uses to describe himself such as fast, smart, heavy, gregarious, and so on. The affective component is usually called self-esteem and refers to how the individual feels about himself. The behavioral component is the tendency to act toward oneself in various ways.

Space does not allow us to consider the more complex structure of the self, nor its measurement, nor how it is formed. Instead we shall focus on the relationship between participation in sport and physical activity and self-esteem. One approach has been to determine the relationship between self-esteem and one's physical appearance. Zion (1965), for example, found that individuals had a significant positive relationship between self-esteem and their conception of their body. Also Felker (1968) observed that endomorphic boys had less self-esteem than meso-morphic or ectomorphic boys. They also found that boys whose fathers had a greater interest in sport had higher evaluations of themselves.

Recently, Hellison (1970) reviewed the literature addressed to the self-attitude–physical activity relationship. Although the lack of research (particularly sound research) limits the conclusions, some tentative relationships were noted. Hellison suggested that physical education programs that meet specific needs such as fitness or remedial programs have greater chances of modifying self-esteem. Also he suggested that activities requiring aggressiveness and courage are effective in changing self-attitudes. Read (1969) suggested that competition in sport alone does not influence self-esteem, but that those successful in sport improve their self-esteem.

It appears unlikely that mere involvement in physical education will produce changes in self-esteem, but that the instructor must provide additional impetus for this to occur. Ludwig and Maehr (1967) provide some support for this notion. They had 7th and 8th grade boys perform simple physical skills in front of a physical development expert. The expert either responded positively or negatively to the boys' performance. Boys receiving approval increased their self-esteem and their preference for similar physical activities. Disapproval, in general, produced the opposite effect.

Our attitude about ourself is perhaps the most important in our constellation of attitudes. Although we have learned that physical education activities may in part influence the self, it is obvious that many other factors may have similar if not greater impact on the formation and change of our self-attitude. But this does not deny the importance of the self-attitude to physical educators, nor does it deny its impact on behavior in general. The self-attitude is important because it in part influences our goals and our behavior in reaching these goals. It is important also because negative feelings toward the self will predispose one negatively toward others.

More attention should be directed at finding the role that

physical education programs (including fitness programs and organized athletic programs) play in forming or changing the self-concept. In other words, how does physical education as a socialization agency influence the development or modification of the self-concept? Also, it would be useful to know how the self-attitude predisposes individuals toward certain types of physical activities, and their performance in these activities. Although we have suggested that through certain structured programs self-esteem can be increased, it is also possible to raise self-esteem to an undesirable level. Too much praise or recognition, too much success, may create an overconfident prima donna who is unbearable to his associates. An important question for investigation is to determine to what extent our present athletic programs create such types.

Practical Applications of Attitude Research

Just as attitude research in psychology received impetus from practical concerns, so has research on attitudes in physical education. Major issues of concern to social psychologists have been with attitudes toward various races and ethnic groups, attitudes toward political issues, and changing attitudes toward foods, smoking, and the environment. In physical education we have been concerned with human conservation by changing attitudes toward the self, maintaining body functions through physical fitness, and satisfying psychological needs.

One of the popular notions associated with sport a few years ago was the lack of prejudice shown by athletes; through sport and physical activity, individuals learned to be tolerant of ethnic and racial groups with whom they affiliated. Prejudice is really only a premature attitude. A prejudice describes an "unusually premature judgment on the basis of extremely restrictive amounts or selective sources of information." (McDavid and Harari, 1968, p. 177.)

Little research has been completed on prejudice in sport. A study by Ibrahim (1968), however, revealed that no difference existed between athletes and nonathlete students in attitudes toward blacks and Jews. The scales used, however, were not validated. As noted in Sheehan's study, we have little reason to suspect that mere participation should lead to the reduction of prejudice toward ethnic groups, but only through guidance by the teacher or coach who uses procedures known to form or modify attitudes, will such changes occur. Thus, physical educators involved in attitude research would serve their profession better if instead of assessing present attitudes, they would address the issue of how attitudes are formed and are changed when participating in physical education programs.

Finally, we should reiterate that attitudes are only one determinant of behavior. By knowing a person's attitude toward an object we cannot predict with a high degree of accuracy his actual behavior. Attitude is not a necessary or sufficient cause of behavior, but it is a contributing cause. Earlier we said that behavior is not only determined by attitudes but also by norms, habits, and expectations about reinforcement. Furthermore, behavior is situationally determined. For example, Holman (1956) found that students' attendance at a football game could be predicted only moderately by knowing students' attitudes about attending football games. However, when students took into consideration other factors that influenced their attendance, their prediction of attendance compared to actual attendance was much higher. Moreover, an even more successful prediction of attendance was obtained when these other factors were combined with their attitude toward football.

CHAPTER 10 SPORT PERSONOLOGY

Attitude and personality are not unrelated concepts. Your attitudes and values form important dimensions of your personality. Similarly, components of your personality will in part determine the development and change of your attitudes. Personality and attitudes, however, are certainly not synonymous concepts—personality is much broader. We use the term *personality* to refer to each individual's uniqueness. A person's particular constellation of attitudes is one unique part, but personality also includes a person's values, interests, motives, and many other factors. Both concepts, attitude and personality, are needed to understand our social structure, and thereby their development through the socialization process.

To be a socially competent person requires the development of society-approved personality dispositions. Obviously, development of positive personality characteristics is a major objective of the socialization process. In this chapter we will be concerned with determining the influence that participation in physical activity, particularly sport, has on the personality and also on how personality factors may influence participation and performance. Initially it will be helpful to understand the structure and process of personality as viewed by the social psychologist. Then we will take a very close look at the existing sport personality research, which is rather extensive.

PERSONALITY STRUCTURE

Hollander (1967) has stated that personality is "the sum total of an individual's characteristics which make him unique" (p. 274). He has suggested that personality may be viewed at three distinct levels and along two dimensions (see Figure 10.1). The three separate but related levels of personality are: (1) the psychological core, (2) typical responses, and (3) role-related behaviors. The psychological core of your personality includes your attitudes and values, your interests and motives, and, of considerable significance—your self-concept. Typical responses are learned modes of adjustment to the environment. By typical responses the personologist is referring to your characteristic manner in responding to such things as frustration, humor, and anxieties. Role-related behavior is the behavior we engage in based upon our perception of a social position in which we are placed.

Among these three levels of personality we can distinguish between an internal and external level. The psychological core of the person is the internal level, and both the typical responses and role-related behavior are at the external or behavioral level. Because the external features of personality are subject to greater influence by the social environment, we find that the external features are more subject to change and the internal features are more stable. Both stability and change (dynamic

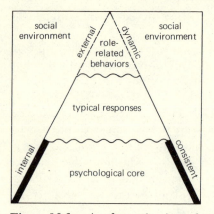

Figure 10.1. A schematic view of personality structure.

component) are desirable. The dynamic component allows for changes based on learning, and the stability aspect of personality provides the needed structure for the individual to function in society.

This conceptual model of personality is illustrated in Figure 10.1. The triangle represents an individual's personality in relation to the social environment within which the person functions. The internal-external and consistent-dynamic dimensions of the personality are represented by two sides of the triangle. For both dimensions the density of the lines represents the permeability that each level of personality has with respect to the social environment. Finally, the wavy lines between the three levels of personality illustrate that the three levels are closely interrelated.

Two strategies of research have been prevalent in the personality area. The first is known as the *nomothetic* approach, which places emphasis on particular personality traits studied in many persons in order to make generalizations about how such traits determine behavior of people in general. The second approach is the *idiographic* approach, which is a detailed examination of an individual in order to make generalizations about him in a variety of life contexts. Thus the idiographic approach tries to study the whole personality and the nomothetic tries to isolate one or several properties of personality in order to establish general principles of personality functioning.

We will not consider further the idiographic approach in this chapter because we are primarily interested in learning about generalizations. Furthermore, very little has been done in sport using the idiographic approach, with perhaps the most notable exceptions being the work of Beisser (1967).

The major thrust of personality research has been at the "typical response" level. In this research the approach has been to describe an individual's behavior and then to ascribe the behavior to underlying forces, such as instincts. This traditional approach, known as "trait psychology," simply looks for consistencies in behavior. In discussing the concept of trait, G. W. Allport (1966) has said: "Our initial observation of behavior is only in terms of adverbs of action: John behaves aggressively. Then an adjective creeps in: John has an aggressive disposition. Soon a heavy substantive arrives . . . : John has a trait of aggression. The result is the fallacy of misplaced concreteness" (p. 1).

Among the best known trait typologies are extroversion and introversion. Such trait typologies, however, ignore the person's interaction with his environment. That is, an extrovert behaves in an extroverted way all the time, regardless of the situation. As might be expected, the trait approach has not been very fruitful in predicting behavior, and has little support among personologists today. Replacing the trait approach, contemporary personology is more concerned with the person's *dispositions*, which refer to tendencies to act or react in certain ways (typical responses) rather than focusing on the response alone. Dispositions intervene between the person's psychological field and his response to the social environment. The disposition approach focuses on the relationship between the individual's psychological core and his perception of a specific situation.

As noted, trait psychology has fallen into disrepute but the term is still frequently used today and similar methods as were used to measure traits are used to assess dispositions. Confusingly, many psychologists today use the term *trait* to refer to dispositions, but a few still use the term *trait* in its former meaning. The difference between the new trait or dispositional personologists and the old trait psychologists is not in how personality is measured but in the subsequent use of the measurement. The contemporary personologist attempts to determine the processes by which individuals differing on a particular disposition react to various situations. The older trait approach ignores situational variables. Among the dispositions that social psychologists have studied are authoritarianism, dogmatism, achievement motivation, risk taking, internal-external control, anxiety, and social desirability.

The measurement of personality can be conceived in two ways: (1) the measurement of individual attributes or dispositions and (2) the measurement of the whole person with emphasis on integration of the personality. At least four major measurement methods are used, some being very similar to those used for attitude assessment. One method for obtaining information about the personality is the *life history*, which is a chronological story about the main facts of a person's life. Another source of information is the *interview*. Both these techniques are more frequently used in assessing the whole personality. More common to the assessment of dispositions is the use of the *psychological inventory*, which comes in two forms—the objective or structured method and the projective or unstructured method. Almost everyone has taken objective personality tests. They are frequently used in schools and for military personnel. Some of the better known inventories include the Minnesota Multiphasic Personality Inventory (MMPI), the California Personality Inventory, and the Cattell 16-PF.

The prime reason for the development of projective personality methods is the transparency of the objective personality methods. That is, it is fairly easy for the respondent to determine what the examiner is assessing. Thus he can represent himself in a manner in which he wishes others to see him, but does not reflect his true personality. Projective methods disguise from the respondent the real purpose of the test. The best known projective techniques are the Rorschach Inkblot test and the Thematic Apperception test. These tests require the person to respond to some stimulus (often a picture or short story) by telling or writing a story about it. From the response, the personologist infers particular dispositions.

The final method of measuring personality consists of making *direct observations* of behavior. Many observational schemes have been developed, some proving more useful than others. All of these methods have advantages and disadvantages. The life history and interview, and in some cases direct observations, are difficult to quantify. Thus the reliability and validity of these methods are difficult to determine. The psychological inventory is more easily quantified, and thus has the highest reliability. The validity of the psychological inventory, however, is frequently subject to suspect. Therefore, it is apparent that among the weaknesses of personality research is the difficulty in obtaining valid measures of personality.

PROBLEMS IN SPORT PERSONALITY RESEARCH

The study of personality is among the more popular areas in sport psychology. The interest is in part attributable to the recognized importance of personality in determining the behavior of individuals. Therefore, physical educators have sought for some time to uncover the personality factors that lead to success in athletic participation. Additionally, physical educators have long believed that physical education and other physical activity programs are important socialization agencies that develop the personality in a desirable way. Thus many sport personologists have sought to procure scientific evidence to answer such questions as:

1. Do various personality profiles determine the selection of, and success in, certain sports? Or a variation of this question is to ask: Do athletes have different personality profiles than nonathletes? Do successful (sometimes called superior) athletes have different personality profiles than less successful athletes?
2. Does athletic participation influence the personality of the athlete? Does success or failure in sport participation influence the personality? Do specific competitive experiences produce changes in the personality of an individual?
3. Another major category of questions stems from the comparison of personality profiles among certain groups. For example: Do female athletes differ from male athletes in personality? Are there differences in personality dispositions among athletes participating in individual versus team sports? Or contact versus noncontact sports? Or are there differences

among athletes playing particular sports such as hockey, basketball, swimming, and gymnastics?
4. Do individuals with high motor ability have different personality dispositions than individuals with low motor ability?

What answers have we to these questions from the prolific literature specifically concerned with sport personology? Unfortunately, we have very few. Because we know so little but have done so much research, our approach will be to focus on the problems plaguing sport personality research. This analysis is quite critical, but is not intended to be destructive. Instead it is intended to be constructive by assessing precisely the "state of knowledge" at this time and to determine future directions. We are forced to take this approach because knowledge about any phenomenon is no better than the methods used to obtain it. Finally, so much has been said and written about personality and sport that is unverified and contradictory to other sources of knowledge, that some straightforward answers are needed, although they may be disappointing. Below we shall review three classes of problems: conceptual problems, methodological problems, and interpretive problems. We will focus attention on those studies that have used personality inventories assessing many characteristics or dispositions of a person's personality. This represents the large proportion of the research. Later, though, we will comment on the study of specific personality dispositions related to physical performance.

Conceptual Problems
Earlier in this chapter we presented a conceptual structure of personality, albeit it was brief for space reasons. Unfortunately, most personality research in physical education has not been initiated from any theoretical or conceptual framework. Consequently, many critical decisions in studying personality appear to be made on a random basis. A conceptualization of personality as presented earlier requires the investigator to answer such questions as: Is the idiographic or nomothetic approach preferable? Should this particular personality study be done at the internal or external level? Should the study focus solely on the

static or consistent parts of personality, or should the dynamic aspects of personality be investigated—or both?

For several reasons, most sport personologists have failed to distinguish between the old "trait psychology" and the newer dispositional approach. The failure to make this distinction has been the most important conceptual problem in the sport personality research. Sport personologists have failed to recognize the importance of the environment or the immediate situation as a significant determinant of behavior. Sport personologists have persisted stubbornly in their efforts to predict behavior by studying only personality traits, disregarding situational factors. Then too some researchers have attempted to predict behavior solely by studying the environment and ignoring individual differences. Social psychologists have long abandoned the monadic approach (studying only personality traits or only the environment), but most sport personologists have not. To predict behavior more successfully, we must adopt the dyadic approach, which considers the relationship between the individual's personality and the type of situation in which he finds himself.

If sport personologists will accept this position, and the evidence is overwhelmingly in support of it, we can begin to ask a different kind of question than that presently being asked. We will delay further comment on this, however, until we complete our consideration of the conceptual problems in sport personology.

Another area of conceptual confusion resides in the lack of distinction between personality dispositions and personality states. In essence, a disposition is a tendency to respond and a state is an actual manifestation or behavioral occurrence. For example, trait anxiety is a tendency to respond emotionally to a wide range of nonthreatening stimuli. State anxiety, however, is the actual feeling of tension and nervousness. Personality can be assessed by examining either or both traits and states. But the conceptual distinction must be recognized.

All of these conceptual problems originate from two related sources. First, sport personologists have failed to attune themselves to personology in general, thus they have not kept abreast of conceptual developments that subsequently suggest method-ological changes. Second, many conceptual problems would be resolved if sport personologists based their work on theory. No theories that are unique to sport have been developed, and it is doubtful that this would be desirable. Instead a number of existing theories appear to provide the necessary conceptual structure so badly needed by sport personologists. (For further discussion of conceptual problems, see Kroll, 1970; Smith, 1970; Rushall, 1969.)

Methodological Problems

A major methodological problem has been the difficulty in obtaining adequate operational definitions for such variables as athlete, various categories of sport groups, and motor ability (Morgan, 1971). For example, what constitutes being an ath-lete? Does participating in an organized sport program make a person an athlete? Are clubs and intramural programs organized to the extent that their participants are also athletes? Is the person who enjoys playing many different sports, but not under any highly organized program, an athlete? It is very difficult to answer questions about the differences between the personality of an athlete and a nonathlete if we cannot clearly distinguish what constitutes either. Another methodological problem has occurred when determining differences in personality profiles between individual and team sport participants, or combative versus noncombative. Many of these studies have failed to con-trol for the athlete participating in both individual and team sports. Another problem area has been in operationally defining high and low motor ability groups. When studying differences in personality among groups varying in motor ability, the many difficulties in the reliable and valid assessment of motor abilities have led to questionable results.

Another cluster of problems centers on how samples are selected and how the results are statistically treated. We will not elaborate on these problems though because they are quite tech-nical. Unfortunately, however, both sampling and statistical errors have invalidated many sport personality studies.

The measurement of personality traits or dispositions has resulted in many additional difficulties. Personality assessment has been done largely with objective inventories, although a few have used projective tests. These tests are usually selected because of convenience and not on the basis of some theoretical or conceptual frame. Generally, no rationale is given for using one personality test over another, other than it is reliable and valid according to the builders of the instrument. Validation of personality instruments, however, varies considerably with the specific purpose of the test. Thus the selection of personality tests must be made in accord with the purpose for which it was developed. The diversity of personality inventories that have been developed by different procedures and from different theoretical positions, makes it nearly impossible to directly compare results of two inventories. Associated with this problem is the fact that many scales that have been used for measuring normal athletes were not developed for measuring normality, but were used to identify abnormality (for further discussion see Kroll, 1970).

These methodological problems are not unrelated to conceptual problems. Lazarus (1971) has said "Research in personality depends on two types of activities: 1. the evolution of fruitful theoretical concepts about personality and 2. the measurement of the qualities of personality postulated in such theory so that empirical observation and experimentation on the constructs can be pursued and theories evaluated" (p. 153). In sport personality research we have largely ignored the first activity, making it impossible to successfully do the second.

Interpretive Problems

Three different types of interpretive problems have occurred, and the first two are closely related to methodological and conceptual problems. The first interpretive problem is isolated to a particular study. Due to methodological inadequacies far too many studies have lacked internal validity. The most frequent error is one we have referred to in other chapters; that is, inferring a causal relationship from correlational evidence. In personality research this error occurs when an investigator discovers that a relationship exists between, for example, success in football and the personality disposition aggressiveness. From this the investigator concludes that aggressiveness causes success. This conclusion is unwarranted because it is possible that having identified only that a relationship exists, success causes aggressiveness.

If the investigator of a particular study does not make this interpretive error, then those reviewing his work often do. The interpretive errors of reviewers are the second source of problems. In most sport personality studies, because of the lack of internal validity resulting from methodological problems, but also from conceptual deficiencies, generalizations cannot easily be made. That is, external validity is very low. It is confusing to readers of the sport personality literature to have a reviewer recognize these interpretive problems, but present a series of positive generalizations regardless. Rushall (1972), in a critique of many published personality studies, concluded that the internal and external validity of every study reviewed was questionable. Rushall (1972) wrote: "Reviewers seem to accept it as being their duty to relate studies but overlook the stringent rules for doing this. What really exists in the literature is a set of generally unrelated, spurious research results. To relate these is a very dubious process" (p. 10).

The third interpretive problem is confined to the work of Bruce Ogilvie and Thomas Tutko and their personality instrument called the Athletic Motivation Inventory (AMI). Ogilvie and Tutko (e.g., 1971; Jares, 1971) have received wide public acclaim through their assertion that they have been able to identify with the AMI unique personality profiles of very successful athletes. Based on their assertion they offer for a fee to assess athletes' personalities, and from this information they will predict success as well as suggest to the coach ways to "handle" an athlete in order that the athlete may maximize his potential.

The AMI assesses 11 different personality traits, which include drive, aggressiveness, determination, guilt proneness, leadership, self-confidence, emotional control, mental toughness, coachability, conscientiousness, and trust. The construction procedures of the questionnaire have never been published, except that the questions were based on the Cattell 16-PF, the Edwards personal preference schedule, and the Jackson Personality Research Form. (Ogilvie et al., 1971.) Thus it is not known how the items were developed specifically, how the 11 traits were identified, and what the reliability and validity of the AMI is. Ogilvie and Tutko do note that the instrument has been given to over 15,000 athletes.

Because of the success of the AMI, as claimed by its originators and its apparent wide use in athletics today, the evidence to support these claims needs to be examined. Critical to the acceptance of Ogilvie and Tutko's claims would be knowing the extent that success is predicted by these 11 traits and knowing the basis for prognosis of remedial treatment for problem athletes. After extensive searching of the scientific literature, it would appear that the evidence has not yet been presented, although Ogilvie and Tutko (1966) constantly allude to such evidence to support their claims.

Besides Ogilvie and Tutko's failure to provide the scientific community with experimental evidence to support their claims, in perspective to current scientific research in personality, their assertions are extraordinary, particularly when based on the outmoded "trait psychology" approach. Their claim to predict athletic success on the basis of 11 personality traits and to also know how to "handle athletes with personality problems" should be considered the most significant development in all of personology since Freud conceptualized the id, the ego, and the superego. Indeed, if their unavailable research can substantiate their sale of personality assessment and diagnoses, their discovery will doubtless be considered the most remarkable advancement in all of the social sciences in the twentieth century.

In addition, their discovery is even more remarkable in that they fail to make reference to any personality research other than their own. While a small army of personologists painstakingly advance inch by inch in their conceptualization and assessment of personality, and although it is quite clear that situational factors are strong mediators of personality dispositions, these psychologists claim that they are able, with 190 questions, to identify problem athletes and to provide guidelines for remediation for these athletes. This is particularly noteworthy in light of the many problems we have identified in the other sport personality research.

The reason we dwell on this interpretive problem is its possible adverse consequences for coaches, athletes, and the profession of physical education, and its failure to adhere to scientific protocol. If in fact Ogilvie and Tutko's claims cannot be supported, the public is being deceived under the auspices that scientific evidence provides the basis for their prognosis. We must be aware that incorrect diagnosis and prognosis may possibly be detrimental to the athlete. Moreover it is a questionable assumption that a person not possessing the same personality profile as the statistical average of a highly successful group of athletes warrants being labeled a "problem athlete."

Our second concern is that "science is a public affair." Scientific evidence does not become accepted evidence until it is scrutinized by other scientists and replicated independently of those making the initial observations. Ogilvie and Tutko have not made their "scientific discovery" available for others to scrutinize before marketing their product. Certainly we would not allow the marketing of a new drug without having it scrutinized by scientists other than the inventors. Is there any reason not to follow similar checks in the use of psychological tools such as personality inventories?

A DISMAL CONCLUSION?

With all of the problems that sport personologists have encountered, what can we conclude about the research investigating the relationship between personality and physical performance? Why has the literature not been consistent in identifying relationships between personality and physical performance? Ryan said it succinctly when he wrote:

The research in this area has largely been of the "shot gun" variety. By that I mean the investigators grabbed the nearest and most convenient personality test, and the closest sports group, and with little or no theoretical basis for their selection fired into the air to see what they could bring down. It isn't surprising that firing into the air at different times and at different places, and using different ammunition, should result in different findings. In fact it would be sur-

prising if the results weren't contradictory and somewhat confusing. [1968:71.]

Thus we must conclude that sport personality research has not uncovered any generalizations about the relationship between personality and physical performance that can withstand scientific scrutiny. Just based on the sheer quantity of research, this unproductive line of research must indeed present a dismal picture. Rushall sees the status of sport personology like this:

After all the years of research no clear findings are available. Physical education and sports personality researchers are not yet off the ground. It is evident that the investigative process must be restored in new directions, utilizing new techniques and designs adopting theoretically sound bases for each work, and avoiding all the errors of the past. If one had to hazard a guess as to one new direction for research it would be the investigation of behavior patterns which are specific to activity environments. Trait investigations are not the answer. [1972:11.]

But in concluding, perhaps the situation is not as dismal as we have portrayed it. For improved personality research to occur, the identification of errors is the first step toward their elimination. Hyman et al. (1954) have said "the demonstration of error marks an advanced stage of science. All scientific inquiry is subject to error, and it is far better to be aware of this, to study the sources in an attempt to reduce it, and to estimate the magnitude of such errors in our findings, than to be ignorant of the errors concealed in the data" (p. 4). Hence, because there is some recognition of errors by sport personologists, perhaps in the near future we will be able to speak more intelligently about the relationship between personality and behavior in sport. To do so will require new directions.

NEW DIRECTIONS

This section must be entirely too brief to provide satisfactory guidance for new directions, but hopefully it will be suggestive.

To this point we have focused on what should not have been done. Now we need to consider what should be done. The first two points are reiterations of themes developed throughout this chapter.

First, the sport personologists must adopt or develop some conceptualization of the structure of personality and its role in determining behavior. In the first part of this chapter we very briefly presented such a framework. Other conceptualizations exist and may serve the researcher's purpose equally well if not better, depending on the researcher's objectives.

Second, the sport personologist must adopt or develop a theory that guides the formulation of hypotheses used in testing the relationship between personality and behavior in sport. If the theory is broad enough, it may provide the conceptual framework referred to above (e.g., Lewin's field theory, Skinner's operant reinforcement theory, or organismic theory). If it is a smaller theory, however, it may not (e.g., Atkinson's achievement motivation theory, Spielberger's state-trait anxiety theory). Some sport personologists believe it would be more fruitful to develop theories unique to the sport-personality relationship than to borrow existing theories. Some attempt has been made toward these ends by Berger (1970) and Kroll (1970). Others, however, have advocated borrowing existing theories and modifying them as experimental testing indicates. Those advocating the latter position suggest that it is parsimonious to determine if existing theories can adequately predict the relationship between personality and behavior in sport. Furthermore, they point out that measurement instruments are available that are developed for the expressed purpose of testing the theory.

Based on current developments in social psychology it seems clear that specific behaviors can be more accurately predicted by investigating the interplay between an individual's personality dispositions and his specific situation. Research by Endler and Hunt (1966, 1968) has clearly illustrated that understanding the interaction between personalities and situations could lead to better prediction of behavior. Bishop and Witt (1970) also found that they could predict leisure time use more accurately by knowing the interaction between personality and situational variables than by knowing either variable separately. Rushall (1971) also has provided evidence in support of this approach in a football situation.

The success of the personality disposition-situation interaction approach has a further implication for sport personologists. It seems unlikely that this approach can be successfully adopted by studying complete personality profiles that may have many different dispositions. Instead the disposition-situation approach will require studying only one or two dispositions as they interact with certain classes of situation variables. Some of the specific dispositions that have been of interest to physical educators include anxiety, achievement motivation, aggressiveness, authoritarianism, competitiveness, and internal-external control. Although anxiety has received some attention in high and low stress situations (Martens, 1971), most of these dispositions have not been investigated under varying situations.

The predominant mode of personality research in social psychology in the last ten years has been the disposition-situation interaction approach. From this research some very interesting theories have been developed, which could be used by the sport personologists who adopt this approach. Atkinson's (1957) theory of achievement motivation and Spielberger et al.'s (1970) state-trait anxiety theory have already been mentioned. Another interesting theory is associated with internal-external control, which is Rotter's (1954) social learning theory. Better assessment of each of these personality dispositions appears possible because each instrument was carefully developed from the theory associated with it. Thus each scale has some construct validity—a questionable attribute of many of the personality profile inventories.

REFERENCES

Ader, R., and Tatum, R. 1963. Free-operant avoidance conditioning in individual and paired human subjects. *Journal of Experimental Animal Behavior* 6, 357–359.

Allport, F. H. 1920. The influence of the group upon association and thought. *Journal of Experimental Psychology* 3, 159–182.

Allport, G. W. 1935. Attitudes. In C. Murchison (ed.), *Handbook of Social Psychology*. Worcester: Clark University Press, pp. 798–844.

————. 1966. Traits revisited. *American Psychologist* 21, 1–10.

Al-Talib, N. M. 1970. Effects of consonant and dissonant role playing with high or low justification on attitude change toward physical education courses. *Research Quarterly* 41, 467–471.

Anderson, B. F. 1966. *The Psychology Experiment: An Introduction to the Scientific Method*. Belmont, Calif.: Wadsworth.

Ardrey, R. 1961. *African Genesis*. New York: Atheneum.

————. 1966. *The Territorial Imperative*. New York: Atheneum.

Argyle, M., and Kendon, A. 1967. The experimental analysis of social performance. In L. Berkowitz (ed.), *Advances in Experimental Social Psychology* 3, pp. 55–98, New York: Academic.

Aronson, E., and Carlsmith, J. M. 1962. Performance expectancy as a determinant of actual performance. *Journal of Abnormal and Social Psychology* 65, 178–182.

Atkinson, J. W. 1957. Motivational determinants of risk-taking behavior. *Psychological Review* 64, 359–372.

Baldwin, A. L. 1968. *Theories of Child Development*. New York: Wiley.

Bandura, A. 1965. Behavioral modifications through modeling procedures. In L. Krasner and L. Ullman (eds), *Research in Behavioral Modification*. New York: Holt, Rinehart & Winston, pp. 310–340.

————. 1969. Principles of Behavior Modification. New York: Holt, Rinehart & Winston.

————, Grusec, J. E., and Menlove, F. L. 1966. Observational learning as a function of symbolization and incentive set. *Child Development* 37, 499–506.

————, and Walters, R. H. 1963. *Social Learning and Personality Development*. New York: Holt, Rinehart & Winston.

Barker, D. G., and Ponthieux, N. A. 1968. Partial relationships between race and fitness with socioeconomic status controlled. *Research Quarterly* 39, 773–775.

Baron, R. M. 1966. Social reinforcement effects as a function of social reinforcement history. *Psychological Review* 6, 527–539.

Beisser, A. R. 1967. *The Madness in Sports*. New York: Appleton.

Berger, B. G. 1970. Factors within the sport environment affecting athletes' personalities: A conceptual approach. Paper presented at the 2nd Canadian Psycho-motor Learning and Sports Psychology Symposium, University of Windsor (October).

Berkowitz, L. 1962. *Aggression: A Social Psychological Analysis*. New York: McGraw-Hill.

————. 1965. The concept of aggressive drive: Some additional considerations. In L. Berkowitz (ed.), *Advances in Experimental Social Psychology*. 2 New York: Academic Press, pp. 301–329.

————. 1969. The frustration-aggression hypothesis revisited. In L. Berkowitz (ed.), *Roots of Aggression*. New York: Atherton, pp. 1–28. (a)

————. 1969. Simple views of aggression: An essay review. *American Scientist* 57, 372–383. (b)

————, and LePage, A. 1967. Weapons as aggression-eliciting stimuli. *Journal of Personality and Social Psychology* 7, 202–207.

Bishop, D. W., and Witt, P. A. 1970. Sources of behavioral variance during leisure time. *Journal of Personality and Social Psychology* 16, 352–360.

Bonzan, R. T. 1965. Attitudes of university publics toward the contributions of the intercollegiate sports program to general education. Unpublished doctoral thesis, Stanford, Calif.: Stanford University.

Brackbill, Y., and O'Hara, J. 1958. The relative effectiveness of reward and punishment for discriminative learning in children. *Journal of Comparative & Physical Psychology* 51, 747–751.

Brown, J. B. 1970. The influence of a motor development program on the social performance of preschool males. Paper presented at the 2nd Canadian Psycho-Motor Learning and Sports Psychology Symposium, University of Windsor (October).

Brumbach, W. B., and Cross, J. A. 1965. Attitudes toward physical education of male students entering the University of Oregon. *Research Quarterly* 36, 10–16.

Buell, J.; Stoddard, P.; Harris, F. R.; and Baer, D. M. 1968. Collateral social development accompanying reinforcement of outdoor play in a preschool child. *Journal of Applied Behavior Analysis* 1, 167–173.

Burwitz, L., and Newell, K. M. 1972. The effects of the mere presence of coactors on learning a motor skill. *Journal of Motor Behavior* 4, 99–102.

Buss, A. H. 1961. *The Psychology of Aggression*. New York: Wiley.

Cairns, R. B. 1963. Antecedents of social reinforcer effectiveness. Paper presented at the Biennial Meeting of the Society for Research in Child Development, Berkeley, California.

Campbell, D. T. 1950. The indirect assessment of social attitudes. *Psychological Bulletin* 47, 15–38.

————. 1957. Factors relevant to the validity of experiments in social settings. *Psychological Bulletin* 54, 297–312.

Caplow, T. 1964. *Principles of Organization*. New York: Harcourt Brace Jovanovich.

Carment, D. W., and Latchford, M. 1970. Rate of simple motor responding as a function of coaction, sex of the participants, and the presence or absence of the experimenter. *Psychonomic Science* 20, 253–254.

Church, R. M. 1968. Applications of behavior theory to social psychology: Imitation and competition. In E. C. Simmel, R. A. Hoppe, and G. A. Milton (eds.), *Social Facilitation and Imitative Behavior*. Boston: Allyn & Bacon, pp. 135–168.

Corbin, C. B. 1967. Effects of mental practice on skill development after controlled practice. *Research Quarterly* 38, 534–538.

Cottrell, N. B. 1968. Performance in the presence of other human beings: Mere presence, audience, and affiliation effects. In E. C. Simmel, R. A. Hoppe, and G. A. Milton (eds.), *Social Facilitation and Imitative Behavior*. Boston: Allyn & Bacon, pp. 91–110.

_____, Rittle, R. H., and Wack, D. L. 1967. The presence of an audience and list type (competitional or noncompetitional) as joint determinants of performance in paired-associates learning. *Journal of Personality* 35, 425–434.

_____; Wack, D. L.; Sekerak, G. J.; and Rittle, R. H. 1968. Social facilitation of dominant responses by the presence of an audience and the mere presence of others. *Journal of Personality and Social Psychology* 9, 245–250.

Cowell, C. C. 1960. The contributions of physical activity to social development. *Research Quarterly* 31, 286–306.

Cox, F. N. 1968. Some relationships between test anxiety presence or absence of male persons, and boys' performance on a repetitive motor task. *Journal of Experimental Child Psychology* 6, 1–12.

Crandall, V. C., Good, S., and Crandall, V. J. 1962. The reinforcement effects of adult reactions and non-reactions on children's achievement expectations: A replication study. *American Psychologist* 17, 299.

Curry, C. 1960. Supplementary report: The effects of verbal reinforcement combinations on learning in children. *Journal of Experimental Psychology* 59, 434.

Dashiell, J. F. 1930. An experimental analysis of some group effects. *Journal of Abnormal and Social Psychology* 25, 190–199.

Deutsch, M., and Krauss, R. M. 1965. *Theories of Social Psychology*. New York: Basic Books.

Dollard, J.; Miller, N.; Doob, L.; Mowrer, O. H.; and Sears, R. R. 1939. *Frustration and Aggression*. New Haven: Yale University Press.

Edwards, A. L. 1957. *Techniques of Attitude Scale Construction*. New York: Appleton.

_____, and Kilpatrick, F. P. 1948. A technique for the construction of attitude scales. *Journal of Applied Psychology* 32, 374–384.

Endler, N. S., and Hunt, J. M. 1966. Sources of behavioral variance as measured by the S-R inventory of anxiousness. *Psychological Bulletin* 65, 336–346.

_____, and Hunt, J. M. 1968. S-R inventories of hostility and comparisons of the proportions of variance from persons, responses, and situations for hostility and anxiousness. *Journal of Personality and Social Psychology* 9, 309–315.

Epstein, S., and Taylor, S. P. 1967. Instigation to aggression as a function of degree of defeat and perceived aggressive intent of the opponent. *Journal of Personality* 35, 265–289.

Felker, D. W. 1968. Relationship between self-concept, body build, and perception of father's interest in sports in boys. *Research Quarterly* 39, 513–517.

Feshbach, S. 1971. Dynamics and morality of violence and aggression: Some psychological considerations. *American Psychologist* 26, 281–292.

Festinger, L. A. 1954. A theory of social comparison processes. *Human Relations* 7, 117–140.

_____. 1957. *A theory of Cognitive Dissonance*. New York: Harper & Row.

Flanders, J. P. 1968. A review of research on imitative behavior. *Psychological Bulletin* 69, 316–337.

Fraleigh, W. P. 1956. Influence of play upon social and emotional adjustment with implications for physical education. *Proceedings of the National College Physical Education Association for Men*, pp. 268–273.

Gaebelein, J., and Taylor, S. P. 1971. The effects of competition and attack on physical aggression. *Psychonomic Science* 24, 65–66.

Ganzer, V. J. 1968. Effects of audience presence and test anxiety on learning and retention in a serial learning situation. *Journal of Personality and Social Psychology* 8, 194–199.

Gates, G. S. 1924. The effect of an audience upon performance. *Journal of Abnormal and Social Psychology* 18, 334–342.

Geen, R. G., and O'Neal, E. C. 1969. Activation of cue-elicited aggression by general arousal. *Journal of Personality and Social Psychology* 11, 289–292.

Gerst, M. S. 1971. Symbolic coding processes in observational learning. *Journal of Personality and Social Psychology* 19, 7–17.

Gewirtz, J. L. 1954. Three determinants of attention-seeking in young children. *Monograph on Social Research in Child Development* 19(2), (Serial No. 59).

_____, and Baer, D. M. 1958. Deprivation and satiation of social reinforcers as drive conditions. *Journal of Abnormal and Social Psychology* 57, 165–172.

_____, and Stingle, K. G. 1968. Learning of generalized imitation as the basis for identification. *Psychological Review* 75, 374–397.

Greenberg, P. J. 1952. The growth of competitiveness during childhood. In R. G. Kuhlen and G. G. Thompson (eds.), *Psychological Studies of Human Development*. New York: Appleton, pp. 337–343.

Guttman, L. 1944. A basis for scaling qualitative data. *American Sociological Review* 9, 139–150.

Haley, B. B. 1969. The effects of individualized movement programs upon emotionally disturbed children. Unpublished doctoral dissertation, Baton Rouge: Louisiana State University.

Harney, D. M., and Landers, D. M. 1973. Teacher versus peer models: Effects of model's presence and performance level on motor behavior. Unpublished manuscript.

Harres, B. 1968. Attitudes of students toward women's athletic competition. *Research Quarterly* 39, 278–284.

Heckhausen, H. 1967. *Anatomy of Achievement Motivation.* New York: Academic.

Heider, F. 1958. *The Psychology of Interpersonal Relations.* New York: Wiley.

Helanko, R. 1957. Sports and socialization. *Acta Sociologica* 2, 229–240.

Hellison, D. R. 1970. Physical education and the self-attitude. *Quest* 13, 41–45.

Henchy, T., and Glass, D. C. 1968. Evaluation apprehension and the social facilitation of dominant and subordinate responses. *Journal of Personality and Social Psychology* 10, 446–454.

Hillix, W. A., and Marx, M. H. 1960. Response strengthening by information and effect in human learning. *Journal of Experimental Psychology* 60, 97–102.

Hollander, E. P. 1967. *Principles and Methods of Social Psychology.* New York: Oxford University Press.

Holman, P. A. 1956. Validation of an attitude scale as a device for predicting behavior. *Journal of Applied Psychology* 40, 347–349.

Hull, C. L. 1943. *Principles of Behavior.* New York: Appleton.

Husband, R. W. 1931. Analysis of methods in human maze learning. *Journal of Genetic Psychology* 39, 258–278.

Hyman, H. H.; Cobb, W. J.; Feldman, J. J.; Hart, C. W.; and Stember, C. H. 1954. *Interviewing in Social Research.* Chicago: University of Chicago Press.

Ibrahim, H. 1968. Prejudice among college athletes. *Research Quarterly* 39, 556–559.

Jares, J. 1971. We have a neurotic in the backfield, doctor; consulting psychologists at San Jose State College. *Sports Illustrated* (January 18) 34, 30–34.

Johnston, M. K.; Kelley, C. S.; Harris, F. R.; and Wolf, M. M. 1966. An application of reinforcement principles to development of motor skills of a young child. *Child Development* 37, 379–387.

Kaufmann, H. 1970. *Aggression and Altruism.* New York: Holt, Rinehart & Winston.

Kenyon, G. S. 1968. Six scales for assessing attitude toward physical activity. *Research Quarterly* 39, 566–574.

Keogh, J. 1962. Analysis of general attitudes toward physical education. *Research Quarterly* 33, 239–244.

Kerlinger, F. N. 1967. *Foundations of Behavioral Research.* New York: Holt, Rinehart & Winston.

Kistler, J. W. 1957. Attitudes expressed about behavior demonstrated in certain specific situations occurring in sports. *Pro-*

ceedings of the National College Physical Education Association for Men, pp. 55–58.

Klinger, E. 1969. Feedback effects and social facilitation of vigilance performance: Mere coaction versus potential evaluation. *Psychonomic Science* 14, 161–162.

Kozar, B. 1970. The effects of a supportive and nonsupportive audience upon learning a gross motor skill. Unpublished Ph.D. thesis, Iowa City: University of Iowa.

Kroll, W. 1970. Current strategies and problems in personality assessment of athletes. In L. E. Smith (ed.), *Psychology of Motor Learning.* Chicago: Athletic Institute, pp. 349–367.

Lakie, W. L. 1964. Expressed attitudes of various groups of athletes toward athletic competition. *Research Quarterly* 35, 497–503.

Layman, E. M. 1960. Contributions of exercise and sports to mental health and social adjustment. In W. R. Johnson (ed.), *Science and Medicine of Exercise and Sports.* New York: Harper & Row, pp. 560–599.

_____. 1970. The role of play and sport in healthy emotional development: A reappraisal. In G. Kenyon (ed.), *Contemporary Psychology of Sport.* Chicago: The Athletic Institute, pp. 249–257. (a)

_____. 1970. Theories and research on aggression in relation to motor learning and sports performance. In L. E. Smith (ed.), *Psychology of Motor Learning.* Chicago: The Athletic Institute, pp. 327–343. (b)

Lazarus, R. S. 1971. *Personality*, 2d ed. Englewood Cliffs, N.J.: Prentice-Hall.

Lefcourt, H. M. 1966. Internal vs. external control of reinforcement: A review. *Psychological Bulletin* 65, 206–220.

Likert, R. 1932. A technique for the measurement of attitudes. *Archives of Psychology* 140, 44–53.

Logan, F. A., and Wagner, A. R. 1965. *Reward and Punishment.* Boston: Allyn & Bacon.

Lorenz, K. 1966. *On Aggression.* New York: Harcourt Brace Jovanovich.

Lowe, R. 1973. Stress, arousal, and task performance of Little League baseball players. Unpublished doctoral dissertation, Urbana: University of Illinois.

Ludwig, D. J., and Maehr, M. L. 1967. Changes in self concept and stated behavioral preferences. *Child Development* 38, 453–467.

McAfee, R. A. 1955. Sportsmanship attitudes of sixth, seventh, and eighth grade boys. *Research Quarterly* 26, 120.

McDavid, J. W., and Harari, H. 1968. *Social Psychology: Individual, Groups and Societies.* New York: Harper & Row.

McGee, R. 1956. Comparison of attitudes toward intensive competition for high school girls. *Research Quarterly* 27, 60–73.

McGowan, K. 1968. The effects of a competitive situation upon the motor performance of high-anxious and low-anxious boys. Unpublished master's thesis, Springfield, Mass.: Springfield College.

McGrath, J. E. 1964. *Social Psychology: A Brief Introduction*. New York: Holt, Rinehart & Winston.

————. 1970. A conceptual formulation for research on stress. In J. E. McGrath (ed.), *Social and Psychological Factors in Stress*. New York: Holt, Rinehart & Winston, pp. 10–21.

Maehr, M. L., and Sjogren, D. D. 1971. Atkinson's theory of achievement motivation: First step toward a theory of academic motivation? *Review of Educational Research* 41, 143–161.

Martens, R. 1969. Effect of an audience on learning and performance of a complex motor skill. *Journal of Personality and Social Psychology* 12, 252–260.

————. 1970. Social reinforcement effects on preschool children's motor performance. *Perceptual and Motor Skills* 31, 787–792.

————. 1971. Anxiety and motor behavior: A review. *Journal of Motor Behavior* 3, 151–179. (a)

————. 1971. Competition: In need of a theory. Paper presented at the Conference on Sport and Social Deviancy, State University of New York College at Brockport, Brockport, N.Y. (December 11). (b)

————. 1971. Internal-external control and social reinforcement effects on motor performance. *Research Quarterly* 42, 307–313. (c)

————. 1972. Trait and state anxiety. In W. P. Morgan (ed.), *Ergogenic Aids and Muscular Performance*. New York: Academic, pp. 35–66. (a)

————. 1972. Social reinforcement effects on motor performance as a function of socio-economic status. *Perceptual and Motor Skills* 35, 215–218. (b)

————, **Burwitz, L., and Newell, K.** 1972. Money and praise: Do they improve motor learning and performance? *Research Quarterly* 43, 429–442.

————, **Burwitz, L., and Zuckerman, J.** 1973. Modeling effects on motor performance. Unpublished manuscript.

————, **and Landers, D. M.** 1969. Coaction effects on a muscular endurance task. *Research Quarterly* 40, 733–737. (a)

————, **and Landers, D. M.** 1969. Effect of anxiety, competition, and failure on performance of a complex motor task. *Journal of Motor Behavior* 1, 1–10. (b)

————, **and Landers, D. M.** 1972. Evaluation potential as a determinant of coaction effects. *Journal of Experimental Social Psychology* 8, 347–359.

Mead, M. 1961. *Cooperation and Competition among Primitive Peoples*. New York: McGraw-Hill.

Meumann, E. 1904. Haus- und Schularbeit: Experimente an Kindern der Volksschule. *Die Deutsche Schule* 8, 278–303, 337–359, 416–431.

Meyer, W. J., and Seidman, S. B. 1960. Age differences in the effectiveness of different reinforcement conditions on the acquisition and extinction of a simple concept learning problem. *Child Development* 31, 419–429.

Miller, N. E., and Dollard, J. 1941. *Social Learning and Imitation*. New Haven, Conn.: Yale University Press.

Mista, N. L. 1968. Attitudes of college women toward their high school physical education programs. *Research Quarterly* 39, 166–174.

Moore, O. K., and Anderson, A. R. 1969. Some principles for the design of clarifying educational environments. In D. A. Goslin (ed.), *Handbook of Socialization Theory and Research*. Chicago: Rand McNally, pp. 571–614.

Morgan, W. P. 1971. Sport psychology. In R. N. Singer (ed.), *Psychomotor Domain: Movement Behaviors*. Philadelphia: Lea & Febiger.

Morris, D. 1968. *The Naked Ape*. New York: McGraw-Hill.

Myers, A. E. 1961. The effect of team competition and success on the adjustment of group members. Unpublished doctoral dissertation, Urbana: University of Illinois.

Nelson, L. L., and Kagan, S. 1972. Competition: The star-spangled scramble. *Psychology Today* 5, 53–56, 90–91.

Newcomb, T. M. 1953. An approach to the study of communicative acts. *Psychological Review* 60, 393–404.

Nighswander, J. K., and Mayer, G. R. 1969. Catharsis: A means of reducing elementary school students' aggressive behaviors. *Personnel and Guidance Journal* 47, 461–466.

Ogilvie, B. C., Johnsgard, K., and Tutko, T. A. 1971. Personality: Effects of activity. In L. A. Larson (ed.), *Encyclopedia of Sport Sciences and Medicine*, American College of Sports Medicine. New York: Macmillan, pp. 229–236.

———, and Tutko, T. A. 1966. *Problem Athletes and How to Handle Them*. London: Pelham Books.

———, and Tutko, T. A. 1971. If you want to build character, try something else. *Psychology Today* 5, 60–63.

Olson, D. M. 1968. Motor skill and behavior adjustment: An exploratory study. *Research Quarterly* 39, 321–326.

Osgood, C. E., Suci, G. J., and Tannenbaum, P. H. 1957. *The Measurement of Meaning*. Urbana: University of Illinois Press.

Oxendine, J. B. 1970. Emotional arousal and motor performance. *Quest* 13, 23–32.

Panda, K. C. 1971. Social reinforcement: Theoretical issues and research implications. *Psychological Studies* 16, 55–67.

Pessin, J. 1933. The comparative effects of social and mechanical stimulation on memorizing. *American Journal of Psychology* 45, 263–270.

_____, and Husband, R. W. 1933. Effects of social stimulation on human maze learning. *Journal of Abnormal and Social Psychology* 28, 148–154.

Ponthieux, N. A., and Barker, D. G. 1965. Relationships between socioeconomic status and physical fitness measures. *Research Quarterly* 36, 464–467.

Read, D. A. 1969. The influence of competitive and noncompetitive programs of physical education on body-image and self-concept. Paper presented at the American Association for Health, Physical Education and Recreation National Convention, Boston, Mass.

Richardson, D. 1962. Ethical conduct in sport situations. *Proceedings of the National College Physical Education Association for Men*, pp. 98–103.

Roberts, J. M., Arth, M. J., and Bush, R. R. 1959. Games in culture. *American Anthropology* 61, 597–605.

Roberts, J. M., and Sutton-Smith, B. 1962. Child training and game involvement. *Ethnology* 2, 166–185.

Rosenbaum, M. E. 1967. The effect of verbalization of correct responses by performers and observers on retention. *Child Development* 38, 615–622.

_____, and Schutz, L. J. 1967. The effects of extraneous response requirements on learning by performers and observers. *Psychonomic Science* 8, 51–52.

Rosenhan, D. L. 1966. Effects of social class and race on responsiveness to approval and disapproval. *Journal of Personality and Social Psychology* 4, 253–259.

Rosenquist, H. S. 1972. Social facilitation in rotary pursuit tracking. Paper presented at the Midwest Psychological Association, Cleveland, Ohio.

Rotter, J. B. 1954. *Social Learning and Clinical Psychology*. Englewood Cliffs, N.J.: Prentice-Hall.

_____. 1966. Generalized expectancies for internal versus external control of reinforcement. *Psychological Monographs* 80, (1, Whole No. 609).

Rushall, B. S. 1969. The demonstration and evaluation of a research model for the investigation of the relationship between personality and physical performance categories. Unpublished doctoral dissertation, Bloomington: University of Indiana.

_____. 1971. The environment as a significant source of variance in the study of personality. Paper presented at the 3rd

Canadian Psychomotor Learning and Sports Psychology Symposium, Vancouver, Canada (October).

_____. 1972. The status of personality research and application in sports and physical education. Paper presented at the Physical Education Forum, Dalhousie University, Halifax, Nova Scotia (January).

Ryan, E. D. 1968. Reaction to "Sport and Personality Dynamics." In the *Proceedings of the National College Physical Education Association for Men*, pp. 70–75.

_____. 1970. The cathartic effect of vigorous motor activity on aggressive behavior. *Research Quarterly* 41, 542–551.

_____, and Lakie, W. L. 1965. Competitive and noncompetitive performance in relation to achievement motive and manifest anxiety. *Journal of Personality and Social Psychology* 1, 342–345.

Schachter, S. 1959. *The Psychology of Affiliation*. Stanford: Stanford University Press.

Scott, J. P. 1970. Sport and aggression. In G. Kenyon (ed.), *Contemporary Psychology of Sport*. Chicago: The Athletic Institute, pp. 11–24.

Scott, P. M. 1953. Attitudes toward athletic competition in elementary schools. *Research Quarterly* 24, 352–361.

Seidman, D.; Bensen, S. B.; Miller, I.; and Meeland, T. 1957. Influence of a partner on tolerance for self-administered electric shock. *Journal of Abnormal and Social Psychology* 54, 210–212.

Shaw, M. E., and Costanzo, P. R. 1970. *Theories of Social Psychology*. New York: McGraw-Hill.

Sheehan, T. 1956. Attitudes of senior male students at Ohio State concerning the athlete and intercollegiate competition. Unpublished master's thesis, Columbus: The Ohio State University.

_____. 1965. The construction and experimental evaluation of a teaching model for attitude formation and change through physical education activities. Unpublished doctoral dissertation, Columbus: The Ohio State University.

Sheffield, F. D. 1961. Theoretical considerations in the learning of complex sequential tasks from demonstration and practice. In A. A. Lumsdaine (ed.), *Student Response in Programmed Instruction*, Washington, D.C.: National Academy of Science-National Research Council, pp. 13–32.

Sherif, C. W. 1971. The social context of competition. Paper presented at the Conference on Sport and Social Deviancy, State University of New York at Brockport (December).

_____. 1972. Females in the competitive process. Paper presented to Women and Sport: A National Research Conference, The Pennsylvania State University, University Park (August 15).

Sherif, M., and Sherif, C. W. 1953. *Groups in Harmony and Tension*. New York: Harper & Row.

Shortell, J., Epstein, S., and Taylor, S. P. 1970. Instigation to aggression as a function of degree of defeat and capacity for massive retaliation. *Journal of Personality* 38, 313–328.

Singer, R. N. 1965. Effect of spectators on athletes and non-athletes performing a gross motor task. *Research Quarterly* 36, 473–482.

————. 1968. *Motor Learning and Human Performance*. New York: Macmillan.

————. 1970. Effect of an audience on performance of a motor task. *Journal of Motor Behavior* 2, 88–95.

Smith, C. P. 1969. The origin and expression of achievement-related motives in children. In C. P. Smith (ed.), *Achievement-related Motives in Children*. New York: Russell Sage, pp. 102–150.

Smith, G. 1971. Violence and sport. *Journal of Health, Physical Education, and Recreation* 42, 45–47.

Smith, L. E. 1970. Personality and performance research—new theories and directions required. *Quest* 13, 74–83.

Spielberger, C. D., Gorsuch, R. L., and Lushene, R. E. 1970. *The State-trait Anxiety Inventory*. Palo Alto, Calif.: Consulting Psychologists Press.

Stevenson, H. W. 1961. Social reinforcement with children as a function of CA, sex of E, and sex of S. *Journal of Abnormal and Social Psychology* 63, 147–154.

————. 1965. Social reinforcement of children's behavior. In L. P. Lipsitt and C. C. Spiker (eds.), *Advances in Child Development and Behavior*, vol. 2. New York: Academic, pp. 97–126.

Storr, A. 1968. *Human Aggression*. New York: Atheneum.

Stubbs, F. 1957. A study of the attitudes of university freshmen male students toward athletes and athletics. Unpublished doctoral thesis, Columbus: The Ohio State University.

Sutton-Smith, B., Roberts, J. M., and Kozelka, R. M. 1963. Game involvement in adults. *Journal of Social Psychology* 60, 15–30.

Swingle, P. G. 1969. Effects of the win-loss ratio and challenge on speed in a two-person lever-pressing race. *Journal of Experimental Psychology* 80, 542–547.

Taylor, S., and Epstein, S. 1967. Aggression as a function of the interaction of the sex of the aggressor and the sex of the victim. *Journal of Personality* 35, 474–486.

Thomas, P. 1969. Interrelationships among physical fitness, selected aspects of mental ability, socioeconomic status, and co-curricular participation. Paper presented at the American

Association of Health, Physical Education and Recreation National Convention, Boston, Mass.

Thurstone, L. L. 1928. Attitudes can be measured. *American Journal of Sociology* 33, 529–554.

Travers, R. M. W. 1972. *Essentials of Learning*, 3d ed. New York: Macmillan.

Travis, L. E. 1925. The effect of a small audience upon eye-hand coordination. *Journal of Abnormal and Social Psychology* 20, 142–146.

Triandis, H. C. 1964. Exploratory factor analyses of the behavioral component of social attitudes. *Journal of Abnormal and Social Psychology* 68, 420–430.

————. 1971. *Attitude and Attitude Change*. New York: Wiley.

Triplett, N. 1898. The dynamogenic factors in pacemaking and competition. *American Journal of Psychology* 9, 507–533.

Ulrich, R. 1966. Pain as a cause of aggression. *American Zoologist* 6, 643–662.

Vaught, G. M., and Newman, S. E. 1966. The effects of anxiety on motor-steadiness in competitive and noncompetitive conditions. *Psychonomic Science* 6, 519–520.

Veroff, J. 1969. Social comparison and the development of achievement motivation. In C. P. Smith (ed.), *Achievement-related Motives in Children*. New York: Russell Sage, pp. 46–101.

Walker, E. L. 1967. *Conditioning and Instrumental Learning*. Belmont, Calif.: Brooks-Cole.

Walters, R. H. 1966. Implications of laboratory studies of aggression for the control and regulation of violence. *The Annals* 364, 60–72.

Wankel, L. M. 1969. The interaction of competition and ability levels in the performance and learning of a motor task. Unpublished master's thesis, Edmonton: University of Alberta.

Wear, C. L. 1951. The evaluation of attitude toward physical education as an activity course. *Research Quarterly* 22, 114–126.

————. 1955. Construction of equivalent forms of an attitude scale. *Research Quarterly* 26, 113–119.

Webb, E. J.; Campbell, A. T.; Schwartz, R. D.; and Sechrest, L. 1966. *Unobtrusive Measures: Nonreactive Research in the Social Sciences*. Chicago: Rand McNally.

Weinstein, E. A. 1969. The development of interpersonal competence. In D. A. Goslin (ed.), *Handbook of Socialization Theory and Research*. Chicago: Rand McNally, pp. 753–775.

Whittemore, J. C. 1924. Influence of competition on performance: An experimental study. *Journal of Abnormal and Social Psychology* 19, 236–253.

Wodtke, K. H., and Brown, B. R. 1967. Social learning and imitation. *Review of Educational Research* 37, 514–538.

Worthy, M., and Markle, A. 1970. Racial differences in reactive versus self-paced sports activities. *Journal of Personality and Social Psychology* 16, 439–443.

Young, J. C. 1969. A comparison of motor performance by preschool children from middle and lower economic groups. Unpublished master's thesis, College Park: University of Maryland.

Young, M. L. 1970. Personal-social adjustment, physical fitness, attitude toward physical education of high school girls by socioeconomic level. *Research Quarterly* 41, 593–599.

Zajonc, R. 1965. Social facilitation. *Science* 149, 269–274.

————, and Sales, S. M. 1966. Social facilitation of dominant and subordinate responses. *Journal of Experimental Social Psychology* 2, 160–168.

Zentall, T. R., and Levine, J. M. 1972. Observational learning and social facilitation in the rat. *Science* 178, 1220–1221.

Zillmann, D., Katcher, A. H., and Milavsky, B. 1972. Excitation transfer from physical exercise to subsequent aggressive behavior. *Journal of Experimental Social Psychology* 8, 247–259.

Zion, L. C. 1965. Body concept as it relates to self-concept. *Research Quarterly* 36, 490–495.

INDEX

75 76 77 7 6 5 4 3 2 1